FROM
CAMBRIDGE
TO THE
WORLD

FROM
CAMBRIDGE
TO THE
WORLD

125 years of student witness

OLIVER R. BARCLAY
and
ROBERT M. HORN

Inter-Varsity Press

INTER-VARSITY PRESS
38 De Montfort Street, Leicester LE1 7GP, England
Email: ivp@uccf.org.uk
Website: www.ivpbooks.com

First published 1977 under the title *Whatever happened to the Jesus Lane lot?*
Revised and expanded edition published 2002 under the title *From Cambridge
to the World.*

British Library Cataloguing in Publication Data
A catalogue record for this book is available from the British Library.

ISBN 0–85111–499–7

Set in Garamond
Typeset in Great Britain by Avocet Typeset, Brill, Aylesbury, Bucks
Printed and bound in Great Britain by Omnia Books Ltd, Glasgow

*Inter-Varsity Press is the publishing division of the Universities and Colleges
Christian Fellowship (formerly the Inter-Varsity Fellowship), a student movement
linking Christian Unions in universities and colleges throughout Great Britain,
and a member movement of the International Fellowship of Evangelical Students.
For more information about local and national activities write to UCCF,
38 De Montfort Street, Leicester LE1 7GP, email us at email@uccf.org.uk,
or visit the UCCF website at www.uccf.org.uk.*

Contents

Foreword

The authors of this fascinating account, though themselves part of the story they tell, have chosen a self-effacing style (see, for example, the modest endnote number 60, on page 235). Perhaps the writer of a foreword can be more personal . . .

'Pembroke College, please,' I said to the taxi-driver at Cambridge station early one evening in October 1944. I had been travelling by slow and crowded wartime trains most of the day (with the inevitable long wait at Bletchley) and was thankful to be at last in Cambridge. I had never set foot in the city before – no preliminary visits, no interview of any kind – and wondered what to expect as I peered through the windows of the taxi at these unfamiliar suburban streets. I was seventeen, and should have been still at school; but the end of the war was in sight and Pembroke could offer me a place immediately, or not for some years to come. Dr B. F. C. Atkinson ('Basil'), who soon befriended me, used to say, 'Timothy came up with a green ration-book' – a document which in those days provided free orange juice for the under-fives.

I was an ordinand since my early schooldays, and Wilfred Knox, the college chaplain, soon sought me out; but it was the CICCU that really welcomed me to

Cambridge, strengthened the roots of my personal faith in Christ, taught me the meaning of fellowship, and introduced me to the Bible as a living book. At their preterminal conference in the elegant Old Combination Room at Trinity, God renewed his call upon my life and his promise to be with me.

Later I recall hearing Bishop J. R. S. Taylor addressing some gathering in Cambridge. 'I warmly commend the CICCU to you,' he said, 'speaking as a parent, a former headmaster and principal of a theological college, and as a diocesan bishop.' It heartened me at the time, since I was only too well aware that the CICCU, though earning a grudging respect from the fair-minded, was never popular with the authorities either of the university or of the mainstream churches. It secures a few references (how could it not?) in Christopher Brooke's admirable 650-page *History of the University of Cambridge*, vol. IV, *1870–1990*, but they are lacking in warmth and appear regretful of the CICCU's stand for a theologically conservative evangelicalism. For a truer appreciation of what it offered in biblical teaching, in mutual encouragement to serious discipleship and commitment, and in the experience (and fun) of Christian friendship, an insider's view is needed. That is the strength of this present account, as of John Pollock's earlier *A Cambridge Movement*.

I value therefore this unexpected opportunity to acknowledge my personal debt to the CICCU, which sustained me, almost as a second family, through six years in Cambridge; and, in what it gave me, has helped to shape all my life and ministry. John Stott spoke for many when he described his own experience: 'I sometimes wonder on which particular scrapheap I would be today, if it had not been for God's providential gift of the UCCF. For I went up to Cambridge a very wobbly and vulnerable young Christian. I could easily have been overwhelmed by the world, the flesh and the devil. But the Christian Union brought me friendships, teaching, books and opportunities for service, which all helped me to stand firm and grow up. I am profoundly grateful.'

This is not therefore a story of merely academic interest for those of a historical cast of mind. It contains lessons and insights that apply as much today as ever. Read on!

Timothy Dudley-Smith
Ford, December 2001

Preface

Without doubt God has done a remarkable work in Cambridge University over 125 years. This book attempts to record that story and some of its worldwide repercussions.

There is no obvious human reason why God should have started and sustained this work over such a long period – after all, as the narrative points out, it has had 125 changes of leadership in that time. The students involved were every bit as young, imperfect and fallible as any other students. The CICCU has never been a 'model' CU and has had its share of problems, failures and setbacks. Nevertheless, in Cambridge as elsewhere, God's providence and astonishing mercy have been fresh year after year to successive generations of students.

The origins of the CICCU go back fifty years before its formal start in 1877, for in 1827 'The Jesus Lane lot' were its forerunners. When the CICCU completed the first hundred years of its life in 1977, chapters 1 to 9 of this present book appeared as its centenary history under the title *Whatever Happened to the Jesus Lane Lot?* At that point it was possible to consult some whose memories extended back before 1900 and a large number whose records and memories were still fresh from 1919 onwards.

When the 125th anniversary was approaching, the

CICCU mooted the idea of covering the story up to 2002, which the closing three chapters seek to do. In a longer work it would have been possible to give far more detail and to follow up the subsequent lives of many more of the CICCU's members. However, in a short book the authors have tried to discern the story's most characteristic features and those of the greatest interest and ongoing benefit.

A list of acknowledgments appears at the end of the book, but we want particularly to thank J. C. Pollock, who allowed completely free use of the material in his book *A Cambridge Movement*. Chapters 10–12 owe a huge debt to Laura Howarth, who did the basic research into the CICCU records and archives for 1977–2002. The project would never have been finished without her help. (Her story appears on page 175.) She died on 23 January 2002, but her work lives on.

The later and junior author counts it a great privilege to make a minor contribution to a book by one to whom he owes so much as a former colleague, a wise Barnabas and a continuing friend. As students both authors received infinitely more in and through the CICCU than they ever gave. They have written with a profound sense of thankfulness to God for his mercies over these 125 years, mercies that will endure for ever.

The distant events of 1877 feel like history; the nearer events of 2002 do not. Yet they are all part of the history that God is unveiling as he takes his gospel forward. May CICCU continue to play its part in that story as an instrument in his hands to make his message known.

Chapter 1
Beginnings

The University of Cambridge in the 1870s was a typically Victorian middle-class institution. Outwardly it was religious. College chapel services (conducted strictly in accordance with the Church of England Prayer Book) were compulsory twice on Sunday and several times during the week. There was great respect for the hierarchy of church and university. Nearly all the students accepted in general terms that Christianity was true – at least *probably true* – though they were not very inclined to do anything about it.

Most students were wealthy and had an assured future of influence and leisure, though there were a number preparing for the Church of England ministry who were sometimes very short of money. If so, they were usually looked down on by the rest. For the majority life was easy-going, sociable, dominated by sport rather than work and, for those who could afford it, there was horse racing with betting at Newmarket, only 15 miles away. It was all very charming, formally rather religious but in reality thoroughly materialistic. Spiritual ambition did not usually survive the pressure for long and many from evangelical homes were lost from a vital faith and drifted into respectable, harmless, self-centred mediocrity.

The founding of a student-led Christian Union in 1877 was therefore a mildly shocking affair. It seemed to be taking religion too far and to have the mark of disrespect for ordained leadership and duly constituted authority. Certainly it needed a lot of discussion before it was decided to go ahead, but since no-one regarded it exactly as a historic event, it passed without much comment at the time.

The Cambridge Inter-Collegiate Christian Union (always called CICCU) did not arise fully formed out of nothing, however. By 1877 Cambridge had had a considerable period of evangelical influence. There was still much prejudice against religious 'enthusiasm', but the violent opposition of earlier times had weakened.

Simeon and Milner

In 1780, 100 years earlier, prejudice had been almost universal. At Oxford and at Cambridge, both strongholds of the Church of England, the fear of Methodist or other Free Church influence had been extreme. Students' papers were carefully vetted before they were accepted, and those suspected of definite evangelical sympathies were usually eliminated. In 1768 six students had been expelled from St Edmund Hall, Oxford, on trumped-up charges when they had been found meeting for Bible study. Others were expelled later for being 'tainted with Methodistical principles' and that university earned a reputation for being, if anything, even more hostile to vital faith than Cambridge. At the time these were the only two universities in England and all students had to agree to the Thirty-nine Articles of the Church of England before admission. Free Churchmen of principle had to go to Scotland for study until University College London was opened in 1828 and Oxford and Cambridge were fully opened to others in 1871.[1] Evangelical[2] faith was virtually unrepresented in the university scene of 1780 by students or 'seniors'.[3]

This stranglehold of a formal religion was broken at Cambridge by two men in a partnership of spiritual and secular influence that was a promise of things to come. Charles Simeon (1759–1836) came up to King's College from Eton in 1779. He was not specially religious, but in his first week received a notice to say that it was compulsory for all students to attend a Communion Service. He took this very seriously and was plunged into alarm and heart-searching. He felt that 'Satan himself was as fit to attend as I'.

Simeon was brought to personal faith and peace in his second term through reading a religious book,[4] but apparently knew of no other converted students or like-minded seniors, though there were in fact a few. In 1782, at the age of twenty-three, he became vicar of Holy Trinity Church, right in the middle of the university area, and began immediately to preach in a way that was virtually unknown in his day. In the same year he became a life fellow of King's College and continued for fifty-four years with one of the most influential ministries that Britain has ever known.

Many were converted under his preaching, but he was mocked and ostracized by the majority. When opposition raged and students were even penalized in exams for 'notorious and obstinate Simeonism', he persevered, through much heartache, and built up a core of evangelical students. They came to him for midweek Bible exposition and 'sermon classes' (for ordinands) as well as attending his Sunday preaching. It was said of him that he had more influence than any archbishop. Because fellows of colleges had to be single, he never married, and he also refused all promotion so that he could continue to exercise his ministry to the university. Partly perhaps because he had no human teachers, he developed a plainly biblical approach. He aimed 'never to speak more or less than I believe to be the mind of the Spirit in the passage I am expounding'. He created a new tradition of biblical preaching and teaching and his 'young men' did the same, in their turn, all over the country.

The opposition seems to us today almost incredible. But at that time it was offensive that a man should be so earnest about religion. That anyone should also so condemn all self-righteousness and rely only on the death of Christ was an insult to current religiosity. Even Isaac Milner, the second man in the partnership, had looked on Simeon with suspicion at first. He played a part in Wilberforce's conversion and became Master of Queens' College in 1788. 'I rigorously scrutinized the character and conduct of Mr Simeon, and for a time entertained some doubt of his sincerity,' he wrote. But he became Simeon's staunch friend. In his rather autocratic manner he dominated his college, allowing evangelical students in when it was extremely difficult for them to get in anywhere else. By 1820, when Milner died, Simeon was beginning to be accepted and the university was more open to evangelicals.

Simeon described his aim as 'to humble the sinner, to exalt the Saviour, to promote holiness'. But it was only when people actually got round to hearing him preach that they were impressed. He and his followers were an object of ridicule and angry criticism. An attempt was made to beat him up, and to be known as a 'Simeonite' or 'Sim' was a passport to contempt. In 1786 and 1796, however, and several times more after 1809, he preached a series of university sermons in the university church of Great St Mary (in the usual course of a rota of preachers). Many who came to mock, or to 'scrape' with their feet (and so show their disapproval in the echoing galleries), were silenced and impressed.[5]

A famine hit the town and the district around Cambridge in 1788 and it was discovered that Simeon had been both an organizer of relief and a generous donor (even then practical Christianity made its mark!). In spite of his eccentric ways and donnish manner the town and university began to respect and love him.

When he died in 1836 the shops were closed and about half the university came to pay their last respects. Meanwhile, hundreds of young men had gone out from his influence as missionaries or ministers. When he started there was only a handful of evangelical ministers left in the Church of England; when he died it was estimated that nearly a third of the pulpits of the Church of England were in evangelical hands, and the flow of active Christians up to the university began to increase. By contrast Oxford was dominated by non-evangelical influences and was about to become the focus of the High Church 'Tractarian' movement. Neither University College nor King's College, London, opened 1828 and 1831 respectively, was attractive to evangelicals, and the only other English university, Durham, was an unknown quantity. In spite of the still-dominant influence of a largely formal Anglicanism, Cambridge was the safest place. Young evangelicals therefore tended to come there, if they went to university at all.

'The Jesus Lane lot'

When Simeon died in 1836, he left no student organization behind him. Indeed, such a thing was probably unthinkable in his day. But Holy Trinity Church continued the evangelical tradition and the converts of the new evangelical parishes all over the country came in increasing numbers to Cambridge and attended that church. In this way they got to know one another to some extent, although compulsory college chapel allowed only limited attendance at town churches. Four developments, however, provided major tributaries for the later mainstream of the CICCU, which was to be formed forty years after Simeon's death.

In 1827, following discussion of a sermon by Simeon (we do not know the verse he was expounding), a group of undergraduates started the Jesus Lane Sunday School. Jesus Lane was then a poor district of the town, and continuous relays of teachers in this mission were themselves greatly helped and enriched. A vision for outreach to fellow students had hardly developed – that was supposed to be the responsibility of seniors – but at least 'the Jesus Lane lot' were giving out and learning to express the gospel. Many who later became influential Christian leaders (including B. F. Westcott, the Bible commentator and theologian) taught there and a fellowship of witness grew up around that work. It also helped to start several other small missions, to townspeople and especially to children, in and around Cambridge.

In 1847 a Christian first-year student (i.e. a 'fresher') named Albert Isaacs was visited in his rooms the morning after his arrival by an older Christian and drawn into the work of the Jesus Lane Sunday School on his first Sunday. The two men became friends and in 1848 Isaacs suggested that they should join with others in a definite commitment to pray for one another as they prepared for ordination – the vast majority of the men preparing for ordination in the Church of England at that time went to Oxford or Cambridge. They formed the Cambridge Prayer Union or, more correctly, the 'Cambridge Union for Private Prayer, for Members of the University preparing for the Ministry'. The members agreed to pray for each other for an hour once a month. By 1849 they had 100 members. They never met together, but prayed, among other things, for 'the raising up of a devoted ministry' and circulated an annual report to which members contributed. In 1850 this was opened also to men who were already ordained and it fairly quickly became dominated by seniors and ceased to have much influence among undergraduates. But it was a beginning and showed what student initiative could do.

In 1858 the Cambridge University Church Missionary Union (CMU) was founded with senior help. This met regularly to pray for missionaries, to hear papers given by seniors and to seek to encourage missionary vocation. It was closely linked with the Church Missionary Society, the largest Church of England Society, which had, from its foundation in 1799, been a strong force for evangelical Christianity at home and abroad – not surprisingly, since Simeon and his friends had had a large part in its origin.

The Daily Prayer Meeting

In 1862 the Daily Prayer Meeting was formed. This was also an undergraduate initiative, based on the experience of two freshers who had had such a meeting at school.[6] The school meeting had at first been suspect, but the headmaster, Dr Howson, had been a teacher at Jesus Lane in his day and he encouraged it. The result was that something of a spiritual renewal took place in the school. When the undergraduates called for advice from the most evangelical of the Cambridge seniors, including the then vicar of Holy Trinity Church, they met with nothing but discouragement. The seniors feared 'excitement'. Did the students not already have 'sufficient means of Grace and perfect Liturgies'? 'Such efforts', they were also told, 'are inconsistent with your present position as undergraduates . . . Assuming the propriety of the movement, *you* are not called upon to undertake it.'

One of them therefore consulted Dr Howson again and the other consulted a home vicar, the famous C. J. Vaughan, who had also been a Jesus Lane Sunday School teacher. Both of them encouraged the students to proceed and, in the teeth of senior disapproval, they went ahead 'in fear and trembling'. Twenty men were at the first meeting in a crowded room behind a bookshop in 29 Trinity Street.

Opposition was strong. 'Our prayer-meeting', they wrote six months later, 'has met with the disapproval of many of the most esteemed men in our University.' Ordinary under-graduates, including the sons of some distinguished evan-gelical leaders, called it 'ridiculous', 'awful bosh'. There were never more than thirty present at first. It lasted only half an hour and consisted of two similar sessions, each containing a hymn and a Scripture reading followed by prayer. The informality of men coming dressed to go on to sports seemed eccentric to some observers. It was an exclusively male meeting and continued to be so until the 1940s.[7]

The leaders of the DPM, as it was always called, began to organize a meeting with a speaker once a term and this was frequently evangelistic in aim. Some of the students were eager personal evangelists. 'You must give your whole heart to Jesus,' one of them wrote to a friend. 'Keep noth-ing back. Remember He gave up all for us.' Nevertheless, most of the work was done by men who were already con-vinced Christians when they came up as students. The DPM shared its premises and its membership with the larger Church Missionary Union. It drew up to 100 on Sundays, and the CMU had 226 on their books in 1875 (when the university had about 2,000 members). The fruits of the ministries of Simeon's young men were begin-ning to be felt increasingly in the parishes and there were more committed Christians among the men coming up than ever before. Victorian middle-class home life was deeply influenced by evangelical Christianity.

Student outreach

At about this time, however, a new factor entered the Cambridge scene. In 1871 by Act of Parliament all reli-gious tests were removed from Oxford, Cambridge and Durham. Only when this overwhelming influence of the Church of England was weakened did Free Church families begin to send their sons in any number to the university. The Free Churchmen were inclined, of course, to be at least independent of the ordained Church of England university hierarchy. It is not certain how big a part this mixture of a fresh tradition played, but in Cambridge the influx of men of Brethren background[8] was strong by 1880, and by 1886 offensively strong, to some of the Anglicans in the CICCU. Robert Armitage resigned from the CICCU Committee then because he felt the Brethren were becoming dominant.

Radical Free Church views were being hotly debated in 1880 under the influence of strong Brethren students such as Granville Waldegrave,[9] though he was chiefly an inspiration for positive evangelism and Bible study. Certainly some of these men injected a fresh and perhaps more reckless concern for evangelism into the more stolid Church of England majority. They must have strengthened the insistence on the need for new birth rather than just baptism. By themselves they would have seemed cranks, but the interdenominational mixture they helped to create had a new vigour.

By 1873 an undergraduate, Sir Algernon Coote, could write, 'There was a large number of out-and-out Christian men – leaders, too, in boating and athletics – whose one aim and prayer was the desire to lead other men to Christ.' In addition there were also some men outstanding in the academic field and by now not a few of the younger teaching staff were Christians of like mind; but in the student world of the day scholarship was not nearly so important as sport when it came to social influence or 'leadership'.

In October a small prayer meeting of friends decided that they must do more to win their fellow undergraduates. They booked the largest hall in Cambridge, the large Guildhall seating 1,300, for Sunday 17 November and sent for a well-known lay evangelist, 'Beauty' Blackwood.[10]

He was a man with unusual evangelistic gifts, a Cambridge graduate, and the one through whom Coote himself had been converted earlier. A strenuous effort was made to visit every member of the university. 'I do not mean', wrote Coote, 'that a card was put into the man's door and left there, but the one who had undertaken to ask him went until he found him; whatever the consequences might be, whatever the language used might be, he went until he found him.'

Constant prayer was made. The DPM had a 'Special Requests Book', in which requests for each day were written on one side and any special answers on the other. A much underlined request was 'for a blessing on Mr Blackwood's visit that many may attend the meeting but especially that *souls may be awakened*'. When the day came, the place was packed. It was estimated that well over half the undergraduates of the university were there. There was intense interest. The DPM book had 'For an abundant answer' written for praise opposite the original request, and the further request 'that the impression made by Mr Blackwood's visit may not pass but deepen in all our hearts'. It was the beginning of new life for many and an enormous encouragement to the Christians to come out of their fellowship into bolder and more active evangelism.

The previous few years had seen the impact of the early 'higher life' or 'holiness' movement. This had its excesses, but it awoke many mediocre Christians to new spiritual zeal. Like many 'revival' movements, the experiences involved seem often to have been of new birth for people who previously possessed only the outward form and beliefs of orthodox Christianity. Some overreacted against their past heritage, feeling that it had been little more than a legalistic creed. There was a turmoil of beliefs, including some unbiblical emphases, but it stirred the rather staid evangelical world and gave a new desire for each to study the Bible for himself and to be fearless in obeying what he found there. This led to the Broadlands Conference of 1874,[11] where many Cambridge men were present, and in 1875 to the Keswick Convention and other similar gatherings 'for the deepening of spiritual life'. The number of zealous Christians in Cambridge increased.

Blackwood was invited back to Cambridge for a meeting in the autumn of 1874. He wrote to his wife, 'Great Hall nearly filled. About six hundred. Deep attention for one hour . . . daily prayer meeting attended by seventy downright men – a marvellous sight. Then down to the river to see Boat Race. Great fun. Saw one man who wished me to be hanged . . .' In 1875 there was a more ambitious joint Mission to town and gown. But the climax came in 1876 with a visit by Sholto Douglas, who had been one of the founders of the DPM and was now a vicar in Derby. He met with 200 men the night before for an address and prayer, and preached powerfully on the Sunday. But the important thing was that he stayed for a whole week. No programme had been arranged, but he went round the colleges encouraging the Christians. The week closed with a breakfast conference at the Hoop Inn in Trinity Street, at which sixty guests discussed 'how best to carry on God's work amongst undergraduates by *undergraduates*' (italics ours). After eleven speeches and much discussion the party broke up at midday. They had been persuaded that more help was needed for the informal fellowships that Douglas had visited in the colleges. Something must be added to the DPM and CMU if the evangelistic work was to go ahead.

Within a week a meeting of college representatives had been called in a room on staircase D, Whewells Court, Trinity College. There was much discussion of the numerous problems – not least the snobbery of the university that made it hard for the more aristocratic to accept spiritual leadership from their social inferiors. There was the attitude of seniors to be faced. It was decided to meet again and to plan a larger conference.

Finally on 9 March 1877, four months after Sholto Douglas's evangelistic address, the small Guildhall was filled with about 250 men. Coote was in the chair and Sholto Douglas present. The letter signed by the college representatives and inviting all interested to be present described the object as 'to promote prayerful sympathy between those who are seeking the advance of Christ's Kingdom in the University, and a more entire self-consecration to God's service; to give information generally concerning God's work in the various colleges; and to make suggestions as to the best means of carrying on the work'. Twenty years later R. F. Horton, a student from Oxford (and, incidentally, a Free Churchman) who had been present, described it as follows: 'There comes back to me a sense of rushing life and assured enthusiasm, young men buoyant and even rollicking, overflowing with animal spirits, but still more with the Spirit Divine. I seem to remember some speeches which had the ring of boyish eloquence in them, and the shout of a King in the midst.'

Six days later the committee met to finalize rules of procedure and to draw up a constitution. The committee was to consist of one representative of each college group. Each representative would nominate his own successor, who would be approved by the college group, and the committee would elect the president and the secretary who between them carried the administrative load.[12] It was quite naturally called the Cambridge Inter-Collegiate Christian Union. 'We determined', writes Coote, 'that every college in Cambridge where an out-and-out Christian man could be found should be represented on the Union, one such man from each college to be on the executive committee – and we found such men in sixteen out of the seventeen colleges in Cambridge.' 'Before many terms had passed,' concludes Coote, 'the seventeenth college had also its representative.'[13]

It would have astonished the spectators if they had been told this body would still be strong 125 years later, and that its fundamental beliefs and emphasis would be virtually unchanged. They would have been even more surprised to know that it would play a notable part in the spread of evangelical Christianity through the whole student world and that it would have at least some indirect influence in churches in almost every country in the world.

Chapter 2
1877–1900
University outreach

The CICCU was started in order to maintain and increase the evangelistic momentum that had gathered from the DPM and the other groupings that had preceded it. It arose immediately out of *evangelistic* activity and the sense of need that that created for some ongoing organization. It was born in an atmosphere of prayer and foreign missionary zeal; but it represented something new. It was the natural overspill of spiritual life and it stimulated further life by its corporate activity.

The witness was by students to fellow students. They had seen the need for prayer and fellowship. They had expressed their concern for the poor children of Jesus Lane and the 'heathen' in faraway countries. Now they gave their energies also to their own student community in a new way and did so without losing any of the enthusiasm for those older concerns. In fact, the subsequent history suggests that this new sense of responsibility for university evangelism served in the long run to enrich and not to impoverish the other concerns. It avoided some of the dangers of an introverted fellowship, which threatened at intervals when the evangelistic emphasis grew weak. Today we would say that they were practising the indigenous principle of missionary work, which is that the workers should be people who belong to the community being evangelized. The CICCU leaders, however, had no sophisticated principles of mission. They just got on with their responsibilities as they became aware of them, and the work prospered.

The founding of the CICCU also represented a new confidence. There had been plenty of a rather defensive emphasis on the need to take a stand as a Christian in the extremely 'worldly' society of Cambridge. Now they went over to the offensive and in this context the necessary defensive side of their work took its place more effectively. A biography of the times says that 'it was often a great safeguard in times of enticement to harmful worldly pursuits to be able to say, when invited to go to Newmarket races for instance, or elsewhere, "I have my Sunday School boys to visit or cottage meeting to take, or I have to speak in the Open Air."'[14] To say that no doubt needed courage, but the CICCU had now become more direct. They began to seek to win their friends and not merely to defend themselves from 'enticement'.

Once founded, the CICCU did not lose sight of its aims. During most of these first twenty-three years a university Mission, or other special effort, was mounted every two years and many of the famous evangelists of the time were heard. This tradition did not grow overnight and it owed a great deal to the extraordinary events associated with the Moody Mission of 1882.

The Moody Mission

Early in 1882 J. E. K. Studd, who was the CICCU president and at the same time university captain of cricket, proposed that the American evangelists D. L. Moody and

Ira D. Sankey should be invited to Cambridge. Moody had visited Britain several times and had an extraordinarily effective ministry to all classes of society, though some thought him vulgar. Studd's father had been converted from a totally worldly life through Moody's Mission in London a few years before. His three sons had all been converted through someone associated with Moody who had become a friend of their father's.

Moody, however, was not a university man, not British, and not middle class. His education was slender, he was not physically attractive, and he was not really an orator. His addresses were homely talks lit up by anecdotes, often with a kind of humour that some felt was a little too popular for a serious occasion. To bring him to Cambridge, to the most critical and perhaps the most hostile audience available, seemed to older advisers to be rash in the extreme. As events proved, the older men were right – it was rash. But it was also of God; and the rashness of student enthusiasm – or was it holy boldness? – won the day.

Moody agreed to come and in November 1882 he and Sankey (the singer who usually accompanied him) began a joint Mission to town and university – three services for the town and a late evening service for the students each day. Every undergraduate received a personal invitation, posters were everywhere and special meetings of preparation were held. Handley Moule, one of the senior friends of the CICCU and at that time principal of the new evangelical theological college in Cambridge, Ridley Hall, wrote in his diary, 'Lord, be Thou really with me in this coming anxious, responsible time.'

Of all the ridiculous days, the Mission started on 5 November, Guy Fawkes' day, which was always given over to bonfires, fireworks and clashes with the police. That year it happened to be a Sunday. The first meeting was held in the new, vast, ugly Corn Exchange, with poor acoustics and an atmosphere like a political meeting. Seventeen hundred men in academic cap and gown[15] were counted entering the building, 'laughing and talking and rushing for seats near their friends'. They were in festive mood. The choir – seventy undergraduates of courage ('I would not join that lot for £200,' said one man) – sang hymns as the hall filled up and the audience responded with rowdy songs. Others built a pyramid of chairs. A firecracker was thrown against the window. When the platform party came in they were welcomed with cheers and jokes. The opening prayer was greeted with 'Hear! Hear!' and the first solo from Sankey with 'Encore'. At this point some of the most rowdy were ejected, but disturbances continued throughout the evening – bursts of laughter, loud talking, shouts of 'Well done!' and humorous questions. 'We went meaning to have some fun', said one man next day, 'and, by Jove, we had it!'

Moody, with his broad American accent, had chosen to speak on Daniel, and his one-syllabled pronunciation of 'Dan'l' was a cause of repeated mirth. Nevertheless, through the heckling and disorder, Moody was heard by the majority and his gift of simplicity and clarity (are these usually part of the gift of the evangelist?) subdued some of the rowdy ones. When the chairman (John Barton, the vicar of Holy Trinity Church) invited some to stay and pray, nearly 400 stayed. Moody spoke again, still on 'Dan'l'. When he returned to his hotel and took off his dripping collar, he is said to have remarked, 'Well, Sankey, I guess I've no hankering after that crowd again.'

As for the CICCU men, 'with heavy hearts we took our way to our respective Colleges'. Studd sat down next day to write to the weekly *Cambridge Review* and put in the DPM 'Special Requests Book' for Monday, 'Special prayer is requested that God would over-rule any disturbance that may take place tonight.' On Monday, however, only 100 or so were present in the gymnasium seating 500, where the meetings were held for the rest of the week. It was orderly but depressing. Moody preached on the new birth.

Nevertheless the fruits began to appear. Gerald Lander, one of the fast set and one of the Sunday night rowdies, had commented, 'If uneducated men will come and teach the Varsity, they deserve to be snubbed.' But on Monday he went to apologize to Moody and stayed for a long talk. He was there again on Monday night and, with so few present, Moody went round afterwards to speak to each one personally. He was superb at personal evangelism. It was reported that five men professed conversion on the Monday. On Tuesday there was little progress.

Wednesday started the most astonishing five days the university had seen. Studd's letter to the *Cambridge Review* appeared that morning. As captain of cricket he was respected and his letter therefore carried some weight. He pointed out that the Americans were guests. 'This being the case you may imagine the disgust which I and many others felt when . . . some fifty, or it might have been a hundred, so far forgot themselves and their assumed character as gentlemen' as to create a disturbance. He politely supposed that these members of the university could not have realized the evangelists' position, 'or they would not have treated the guests of some of their fellow undergraduates, who are also visitors to our country, in such a very ungentlemanly way'. After expressing a hope that they would 'come and hear Mr Moody speak and Mr Sankey sing and that by their attention will show how much they regret having so misunderstood the facts of the case', he concluded with a neat suggestion that this would also forestall any criticism that Cambridge men could not behave as well as Oxford men, 'or even as well as those far below them in the social scale'. Also on the Wednesday Moody asked Christian mothers who had come in for the crowded town meeting in the afternoon to stay and pray for the students – 'some mothers' sons'. A hundred and fifty to two hundred stayed for a moving prayer meeting.

The gymnasium that night was still not full, but the atmosphere was far removed from that of the Sunday. As Moody spoke, he could sense that those mothers' prayers would be answered. At the end of the address he determined to prove it. 'I have not yet held an inquiry meeting for you, gentlemen,' he said, 'but I feel sure many of you are ready and yearning to know Christ. When you are in difficulties over mathematics or classics, you do not hesitate to consult your tutors. Would it be unreasonable for you to bring your soul-trouble to those who may be able to help you? Mr Sankey and I will converse with any who will go up to the empty gallery yonder . . . Let us have silent prayer.'

There was a pause. The gallery, normally used as a fencing room, was reached by a steep iron staircase from the centre of the gymnasium. To reach it a man would have to face his friends and acquaintances; and even if they were supposed to be praying, the clatter of the iron steps would open scores of inquisitive eyes. Moody did not want shallow decisions; as he said on another night that week, 'No-one can have really received Christ in his heart if he does not confess Him to his friends, if only by some small action.'

No-one moved. Then 'amidst an awful stillness' a young Trinity man got up, and 'half hiding his face in his gown, bounded up the stairs two at a time'. Soon the stillness was quite gone, as one man followed another up the iron staircase, while the choir sang a further hymn. Mr Moody remarked, 'I never saw the gowns look so well before' and with Sankey and other helpers went up the stair himself. He found fifty-two men in the gallery. Among them was Gerald Lander, the rowdy of Sunday night.

On Thursday the gymnasium was fuller (still under 500). Graduates of all persuasions began to come as well as undergraduates. Moody preached on sowing and reaping, but Sankey began to have influence also. Arthur Benson (son of the archbishop), who did not himself find peace with God, described it as follows: 'An immense bilious man, with black hair, and eyes surrounded by flaccid, pendant baggy wrinkles came forward with an unctuous gesture, and took his place at a small harmonium, placed so near the front of the platform that it looked as if both player and instrument must inevitably topple over; it was inexpressibly ludicrous to behold. Rolling his eyes in an affected manner he touched a few simple chords, and a marvellous transformation came over the room. In a sweet powerful voice, with an exquisite simplicity combined with irresistible emotion, he sang "There were ninety and nine". The man was transfigured. A deathly hush came over the room, and I felt my eyes fill with tears; his physical repulsiveness slipped from him and left a sincere, impulsive Christian, whose simple music spoke straight to the soul.'

Then Moody took over. 'He had not spoken half a dozen words before I felt as though he and I were alone in the world. After a scathing and indignant invective on sin he turned to draw a picture of the hollow, drifting life with feeble, mundane ambitions – utterly selfish, giving no service, making no sacrifice, tasting the moment, gliding feebly down the stream of time to the roaring cataract of death. Every word he said burnt into my soul. He seemed to me to probe the secrets of my innermost heart; to be analysing, as it were, before the Judge of the world, the arid and pitiful constituents of my most secret thought. I did not think I could have heard him out . . . his words fell on me like the stabs of a knife. Then he made a sudden pause, and in a peroration of incredible dignity and pathos he drew us to the feet of a crucified Saviour, showed us the bleeding hand and the dimmed eye, and the infinite heart behind. "Just *accept* Him," he cried; "in a moment, in the twinkling of an eye you may be His – nestling in His arms – with the burden of sin and selfishness resting at His feet." '

On the Friday the gallery up the iron staircase was packed. Over 100 were counted. Barclay F. Buxton, a recent Cambridge graduate who was present, wrote later, 'There and then the decision was made. Christ came and for fifty and more years has been my Saviour, Shepherd and King.'[16]

The climax came on Sunday 12 November. The university meeting was back in the Corn Exchange seating nearly 2,500. It was crowded. It was reckoned that well over half the undergraduates of Cambridge were present – perhaps 1,800 were there, plus graduates and some townspeople. There was no opposition – only rapt attention. Moody spoke from Luke 2, 'The angel said unto them, Fear not: for behold I bring you good tidings of great joy, for unto you is born a Saviour, which is Christ the Lord.' 'The angels called it good news,' he began. 'It was either such or it was not such. If it is good news you certainly ought to be glad to hear it; if it is not good news, the quicker you find it out the better, and dismiss the whole subject!' He went on to speak of the resurrection of Christ, of death, sin, judgment and peace through faith in Christ. 'If the God of the Bible is real, then take your stand, and take it boldly. Don't be religious with religious people, and make sport when with scoffers!' His final theme was 'Seek *ye first* the kingdom of God'.

The lasting results

No-one counted the converts, but about 200 stood on the last night to indicate that they had received blessing during the week. Handley Moule knew of 'scores of true, deep, lasting conversions'. Ridley Hall (the theological college in Cambridge for graduates) suddenly grew in numbers; two years later Moule could say that all his students were men whose lives had been 'influenced more or less by Moody's Cambridge Mission'. Not a few, including Gerald Lander and some others who had been notably worldly and selfish men, were giving generously to missionary work within a few weeks and went overseas later as missionaries. A religious journalist wrote that there was a 'marked increase in the attendance at the Daily Prayer Meeting . . . a higher tone of spiritual life among the men – greater prayerfulness, greater diligence in study'.

Handley Moule started a series of Bible expositions from the Greek text of the New Testament every Sunday after evening sermon and these became a powerful influence for solid Christian growth and the forerunner of the later Saturday night Bible Readings. Douglas Hooper was another Mission convert. He was a former horse-racing enthusiast who had kept his own horse and trap to take him over to Newmarket. He became the founder of the Morning Watch Union. He collected his friends to go to Moule's talks and then got them to sign, 'I will endeavour, God helping me, to set aside at least twenty minutes, and if possible one hour, in the early morning for prayer and Bible study, and also a short but uninterrupted time before retiring to rest.' When be left Ridley four years later to go to Africa as a missionary (where, incidentally, his son and grandson followed in due time), his final words to his fellow students were not, to their surprise, a missionary exhortation, but 'Remember the Morning Watch!'

In 1885 the CICCU started Sunday night meetings in the Alexandra Hall of the YMCA, where students themselves would speak and give their testimonies. The meetings were held here rather than in a church, because the speakers were not ordained. Once more there was a shaking of heads among the older men, but student enthusiasm won; and although the main benefit may have been to the speakers, the meetings were not without fruit. Many students really took a stand for Christ when they agreed to speak at this or at the numerous open-air services held in and around Cambridge. This was also for many the start of a call to full-time ministry.

In the summer term the Alexandra Hall meetings were transferred to the open air – on the 'Backs' behind Clare and King's.[17] These meetings were partly the result of influence from the Salvation Army and the 'holiness' movements of the time. After running for a number of years in this way, outside speakers were brought in instead of students for the Sunday night meetings. The regular Sunday evening evangelistic sermons, which long continued in different places, were thus established. They were still in the open air (often in the market place) during the summer right up to the 1930s, when it was decided that non-Christian friends were really easier to reach through an indoor service. A tradition developed of working and praying earnestly to get friends along to these services and then talking to them personally afterwards. Perhaps at times a CICCU member's success or failure in getting a non-Christian friend along became too much a matter of pride or of legalistic duty. But men were brought to hear the gospel and not a few were converted year by year.

George Pilkington (later of Uganda) was one of the most noted converts of the Alexandra Hall meetings. In his first term four Christian freshmen in his college had systematically called on all the other fifty-two students in their year until they had obtained a talk on spiritual things with each one. 'Pilks' wrote them off as mad and criticized fiercely those who continued to try to get him to meetings. But, once converted, he was as zealous for truth as he had been against it and threw himself into pioneering missionary work as soon as he graduated. A brilliant classical scholar, he was soon involved in Bible translation.

The holiness debate

The Keswick Convention was only one aspect of a turmoil of teaching about holiness that began to have a powerful influence in Cambridge at that time. In the same year as the start of the Alexandra Hall meetings John Smyth-Pigott, a rather erratic former Cambridge man of thirty-three who was now an Anglican curate, came back to Cambridge for a further degree. He and some others with him did not think Keswick went far enough. They taught sinless perfection quite explicitly (i.e. that Christians should expect to be completely free of sin). In the lively discussion about holiness, Pigott, perhaps because he was older and because he was extreme, began to have a dominant influence over some.

Handley Moule and others became alarmed, but the CICCU president, Douglas Hamilton, came under Pigott's spell. Biblical phrases were used in unbiblical ways. Hamilton came to believe that he had arrived at a new state – he was no longer a sinner and now had direct and authoritative guidance from God on the smallest matters. He had to obey this guidance even when it seemed contrary to Scripture. He seemed more spiritual than others.

Such irrational guidance was impressive to some; but leaving the Bible behind led quickly into disregarding its moral commands and the result was a drift into sexual perversion. Moule and Barton (the vicar of Holy Trinity Church) spent long hours helping men caught up in the excesses. Some were revolted and gave up all faith; others pulled out in time. Hamilton joined the Agapemonites, a minute sect whose views were a compound of genuine spiritual desire with immorality and plain heresy. He left Cambridge and with Pigott joined the 'Abode of Love' at

Spaxton in Somerset, where a community built on their astonishing principles of morality existed. In 1902 Pigott claimed that he was the Immortal Messiah.

This was for a few the tragic climax of what had been for a decade or so a deeply earnest striving after holiness. Moule described the period afterwards as a time of 'wonderful life'. More sober leadership took over, though none the less earnest. A series of Moule's 1884 lectures on sanctification had been published in 1885 under the title *Thoughts on Christian Sanctity* and had steadied many. By 1887 the CICCU was set again on a more solidly biblical course. From forty to sixty were at the Sunday early morning Prayer Meetings and 230 or so at the Alexandra Hall.

Open-airs

Open-air work in the villages around Cambridge was a feature of the work of the more energetic. Douglas Thornton (see next chapter) wrote in his diary, 'In the evening off to Trumpington . . . Open air at 7.30. Very clear addresses by Compton on love, Monro on holiness, Hibbert Ware on sin in heart, Woods on redemption, I on acceptance. Three boys I had decided for Christ. Tom Barker had some more. Postman convicted.' Or again, 'Open air on green (at Knapwell) from 7.30 p.m. to 9.30 p.m. . . . "There is a green hill" brought tears to many eyes. Woods on "My Saviour". I had 14 boys who one by one decided in prayer for Christ and to read their Bibles. An old woman got blest . . . Back 9 miles in 35 minutes praising God and running into a Proctor.'[18]

By the 1890s the CICCU was at the height of its influence and popularity. It took courage to join it wholeheartedly, and there were not lacking members who held a rather anti-intellectual outlook – after all, had not Moody been an unlettered man? But there was a place for all kinds. G. T. Manley, who in 1893 became Senior

Wrangler (i.e. the best student of his year in mathematics), described it as follows: 'I entered the University with an idea that evil companions would surround me on every side; a prospect which at that time filled me rather with pleasurable anticipation than alarm. I was disappointed; for in a year I found myself for the first time believing in Christ as my Saviour.'

Manley in turn befriended an overseas student on his staircase – Jan Smuts the South African. In after years General Smuts always treasured a Greek New Testament that Manley had given him. When he was in Britain on important national business he would sometimes ring up the obscure country parson that Manley became after his missionary career. Manley, in fact, was a great stimulant to serious discussion. The CICCU included a Religious Discussion Society to discuss the antagonisms to Christianity and equip the members to meet them. But the CICCU was best known for what C. F. Andrews, then an undergraduate, described later when he was less sympathetic, as the 'open, ardent courage, the passionate fervour' of their devotion to Christ.

At that time they also received fresh pastoral and evangelistic help in the founding in 1895 of the Cambridge Pastorate. Handley Moule was behind the idea and by 1898 there were two ordained men busy full time with an endless round of pastoral counselling and personal evangelism. There was a link with Holy Trinity Church and Ridley Hall, but the Pastorate was essentially an independent ministry to students. For many years it provided tremendous help to the CICCU.

Meanwhile agnosticism was growing and Bertrand Russell was a focus of attention. Those who thought themselves intelligent, as G. M. Trevelyan once remarked, took it more or less for granted that Christianity was discredited. But the task of the CICCU remained basically the same – to win men for Christ. This by the grace of God they did.

Cambridge in the 1890s was still outwardly religious and the CICCU was its dominant spiritual influence. The Anglo-Catholic group revolving round Little St Mary's Church was small, though it attracted some, like C. F. Andrews, who found the CICCU too enthusiastic. The college chapels, although compulsory, were at best dull and 'were going modernist' already in 1892.[19] Many CICCU leaders went into the ministry if they did not go to the mission field. Ridley Hall, presided over by Moule, was a home of true godliness.

The Faculty of Divinity, however, was by then teaching moderate liberalism. Theodore Woods, who had been converted as a fresher in February 1893 in an outstanding CICCU Mission led by the Revd George Grubb, became CICCU president for 1894–5. He had a quite unusual personal influence and was an ardent evangelist of impeccable orthodoxy. His theological studies, however, which he started when he went on to Ridley in 1895, unsettled his views of the Bible. Whereas Moule remained always conservative and taught his men to love the Bible, the faculty taught something different. Woods's biographer wrote, 'Like many other young students at that time he moved slowly and steadily towards' a more liberal view of the Bible. 'This was not without pain and struggle; there were discussions with friends that went on far into the night and stirred many deep searchings of heart.' Like many other ardent and simple evangelists he came out of academic theological study a changed man. No-one had prepared him for it. Even Moule, though he had been Professor of Divinity, was not a very satisfactory guide because he did not really answer the problems.[20]

No-one then knew quite how to deal with liberalism without being swept away, unless they just brushed it aside. In that decade and the next, very few theological students remained orthodox if they worked hard at theology, unless they were the kind of men who were set on learning only what would serve the interests of evangelistic service. The missionary enthusiasts, for instance, remained on the whole much more orthodox than those who stayed at home. This was partly because they were exposed to liberal pressures for a shorter period, but was also a result of being forced to concentrate on the gospel and not having time to drink deeply of the critical spirit. Critical questions seemed irrelevant to most of them.

Chapter 3
1877–1900
Missionary outreach

From the start the CICCU members had a lively interest in overseas missionary work. From its founding in 1858 the Church Missionary Union had flourished and the very influential CMS sent its best speakers to Cambridge. Henry Martyn was remembered with honour. But the Moody Mission and its results were dynamite. During 1883 and 1884 the CMS received a considerable number of offers from men who had been helped or converted in the Mission and other offers came later after ordination.

The Cambridge Seven

Then, in the autumn of 1884, came the 'Cambridge Seven', who not only had an influence throughout Britain but in their turn stirred Cambridge again to its depths. Stanley Smith, the son of a London surgeon, had come up to Cambridge in 1879 a rather insecure and introspective Christian with indifferent health. After one term at Cambridge he came to a deep, personal experience of Christ, largely through the friendship of a fellow student, Granville Waldegrave (see n. 9). 'I decided by God's grace', he wrote, 'to live for and to Him . . . Thank God for sending G. W. here.' He grew in confidence (and in physical strength), and became an ardent personal evangelist and also stroke of the Cambridge boat. He graduated in 1882 and started teaching, but increasingly felt called to missionary service and arranged to talk with Hudson Taylor, the leader and founder of the China Inland Mission (now the Overseas Missionary Fellowship).

C. T. Studd (the brother of J. E. K. Studd) had begun at Cambridge the same year as Smith, but had been playing cricket for England in Australia during Moody's Mission. He had been converted, like his brother, but his faith remained largely lifeless while he was rising to be captain of university cricket in 1883. He was probably the best all-round cricketer in Britain from 1881 to 1884 and his name was a household word in sporting circles, but he was spiritually a nonentity. 'Instead of telling others of the love of Christ,' he wrote, 'I was selfish and kept the knowledge to myself. The result was that gradually my love began to grow cold, and the love of the world began to come in. I spent six years in that unhappy backslidden state.' He was suddenly brought back to reality by the nearly fatal illness of another brother, who in his illness had cared only about the Bible and the Lord Jesus Christ. God 'taught me the same lesson', he wrote. He immediately set to work for Christ, not least among his cricketing friends. Smith, whom he had known in Cambridge, helped him to make progress spiritually and in 1884 they both offered to the China Inland Mission and were accepted.

Dixon Hoste was another member of the group. He was an army officer and had been influenced by his brother, who was at Trinity College, Cambridge, with Smith and Studd. He had also been deeply influenced in the Moody Mission. Dixon had never been at Cambridge himself, but was in fact the first of the seven to offer to CIM.

Montagu Beauchamp was a cousin of Granville Waldegrave and a prominent oarsman. He was in the same year and college as his cousin C. T. Studd and his friend Stanley Smith. Stanley Smith and J. E. K. Studd (also at Trinity College) had met to pray for him every day for a whole term because he seemed at best half-hearted as a Christian. After a while they had their reward and Beauchamp came to a new spiritual experience. Smith could write 'how marvellously changed he is', and together they started a Bible study for members of the college boat club.

William Cassels, another Cambridge contemporary (but at St John's College), was an old schoolfriend of Stanley Smith's. Finally there were the two Polhill-Turner brothers. Arthur had been converted in the Moody Mission. He soon started in earnest to try to win his brother Cecil, who had graduated a year earlier. They had both been members of the fashionable and idle set, occupied with theatres, dancing, racing and cards. The change in Arthur's interests was dramatic. He was quickly drawn into the fellowship of the CICCU, attended the Daily Prayer Meeting, and became a particular friend of Beauchamp. He made his brother promise to read the Bible every morning and after a year or so Cecil became a definite Christian.

All these seven, linked together by bonds of friendship and Cambridge associations, offered to the China Inland Mission and were accepted, although several of them had only recently become personal Christians. When the news broke, it caused a sensation. The CIM was not a well-known society and China at that time was a remote and little-known land. That seven such young men should give up their popularity and extremely good prospects at home to go to such a distant and apparently unimportant work was shattering. That they should do so with such gusto and enthusiasm was profoundly challenging to Victorian complacency. Cambridge in particular was deeply moved and crowded meetings were arranged to hear them speak.

Before sailing, Smith and Studd ('SP' and 'CT') undertook in 1885 an extensive tour of a number of universities. They were always enthusiastically received and had many deep, personal talks with undergraduates. They had a particularly important impact in Edinburgh, where they were persuaded to return twice more to crowded audiences of up to 2,000 students, 'the largest meeting of students that has ever been held'. They had a string of quarter-hour evangelistic talks with individuals all next day. After the first visit a crowd of students went to the railway station to see them off on the night train and demanded another speech on the platform. As the station echoed with resounding cheers, a porter drily remarked, 'Th're a' meedical students, but th're aff their heeds!' After the final meeting in Edinburgh the room was still full at half-past ten with men asking, 'What must I do to be saved?' Some who had been converted at the first meeting were already helping their friends, and when they were turned out of the hall at midnight the work was still going on. They left behind them an undoubted touch of revival.

In Leicester they had a profound influence on F. B. Meyer, launching him on his ministry at Melbourne Hall and later in South Africa. They had asked him, 'Have you ever given yourself to Christ, for Christ to fill you?' Their main emphasis was evangelistic rather than missionary, but their evangelistic message was clearly uncompromising. Smith was something of an orator but Studd, who was a poor speaker, often made a bigger impression by his transparent sincerity and earnestness. A Cambridge student commented, 'I saw that we were to take up our cross and follow Christ: that there was to be no compromise however small, that there was to be nothing between us and our Master.'[21]

Smith and Studd were both aged only 23 at the time and spoke as young men to young men with a power that was evidently of God. The effect was dramatic and it was not a short-lived enthusiasm for them or for many of those they influenced. All the 'Seven' carried out a long spell of missionary work. Stanley Smith's son, grandsons and granddaughters and at least one great-grandson have also been missionaries. But the 'Seven' provided a far more wide-ranging inspiration and a zeal for missionary work that shook the student world and had an influence on the attitude to missions throughout Britain. The spiritual impact of the Moody Mission, the many other evangelistic movements and the growing influence of the Keswick Convention were given a fresh foreign missions emphasis that was to last for a long time. Handley Moule had to plead with his students at Ridley Hall to stay at home!

Continued missionary zeal

The next few years saw this revival of missionary interest maintained in Cambridge. The Church Missionary Society alone had thirty-one CICCU men offer in 1886 and, as late as 1893, 140 Cambridge men offered to CMS in the one year. Over the whole period of the existence of the CMS from 1798 to 1880 it had sent out 156 graduates, of whom seventy-eight were from Cambridge. In the fourteen years 1881–94 there were 170 graduates, 100 of them from Cambridge. Over a quarter of all new CMS missionaries from 1882 to 1894 were CICCU men (ninety-five out of 369) and other societies probably benefited similarly.[22]

In Cambridge itself the missionary interest was strengthened by the formation of 'Missionary Bands' – groups of undergraduates who met, usually weekly, for

missionary study, prayer and raising of money for a particular missionary or field. Occasionally they had outside
speakers; usually they read papers to one another. These
Bands seem to have included between a half and a third of
the CU membership and did much to consolidate and
develop what the 'Seven' had begun. The call to all-out
Christian discipleship from then onwards almost always
included the challenge to consider seriously the possibility
of missionary service, with all the hazards that that
included in those days.

The evangelistic concern also was not confined to overseas or to Cambridge. A series of joint annual conferences
was held with the OICCU (the Oxford Inter-Collegiate
Christian Union) that had been founded in 1881, largely
through the constant encouragement of the CICCU.
Mutual interest and prayer became stronger. Moody had
gone on to Oxford in 1882 after his Mission in Cambridge
and the two Christian Unions developed together. Oxford
University, however, was less well supplied with evangelical
freshers and its official theological leadership was decisively
High Church and more hostile than Cambridge to evangelical Christianity. In the early 1900s an Oxford contingent at the Keswick Convention (including Temple
Gairdner and J. H. Oldham) wrote a letter to the
Convention leaders asking good evangelical families to
send their sons to Oxford. The OICCU then was never so
strong as the CICCU (until the 1960s), but it also produced its notable leaders and missionaries.

Robert P. Wilder

The news of the Cambridge Seven was taken over to the
USA in the summer of 1885 by J. E. K. Studd, who was
invited by Moody to one of his student conferences. This
aroused great interest and helped towards developing a
national missionary movement among students there.

Among other important results of the visit was the conversion of John R. Mott, who came to personal faith in Christ in an interview with Studd the day after he had spoken at a meeting. The moving spirit was Robert Wilder, a quiet, scholarly Princeton student, who in 1886 became the main influence in starting the 'Student Volunteer Movement' in the States. He was very able and a good speaker, but he won his men more by personal friendship and personal conversation, and as soon as anyone was committed to the missionary cause he was persuaded to rope in others also. Wilder was a great man of prayer and was enormously helped by his sister, Grace, who was also a student and a remarkable prayer warrior. They had prayed and worked for a missionary movement since 1883, but it had remained local.

Others had been concerned too and now they prayed for 1,000 missionaries. In the first year, 1886–7, the SVM enrolled 2,106 students, though not all went overseas. One of the earliest to enrol was J. R. Mott. The SVM members signed a declaration: 'It is my purpose, if God permit, to become a foreign missionary.'[23] This was intensely personal. Almost from the start they adopted also a Watchword: 'The evangelization of the world in this generation.' This, by contrast, gave a world-wide vision, which was something new. They did not mean the conversion of the world, but they did mean the evangelization of the world *in this generation*. It gave tremendous urgency to the task and for twenty years the Watchword was to prove a major source of missionary challenge in student circles the world over. Wilder, and then Mott, carried it everywhere in their extensive travels.

We have to remember that the idea of university graduates going abroad as missionaries was rather new. A very high proportion of missionaries had been folk with little education, and to become a missionary was regarded as a step down the social scale – a disgrace to a middle-class family. That any large number of outstanding students should offer was revolutionary. That was partly why news of the Cambridge Seven caused such a sensation in America as well as in Britain. But as an American student put it, 'We had been asleep as to the subject of foreign missions, while this earnest group at Princeton (Wilder, etc.) had been studying the urgent needs of lost souls all over the world, and praying earnestly for them and for an awakening in American colleges to meet these needs.'[24] Revival of Christian life among students and missionary recruiting went hand in hand and their prayers in both directions were remarkably answered. Their preaching combined evangelism with a call to full consecration and to missionary service all rolled into one. So many students were nominal, orthodox Christians and they needed life.

Willingness to go to the mission field became almost a test of the reality and vividness of faith. American Christian student life had been dramatically awakened by this volunteer movement, rather in the same way as the Cambridge Seven had affected Britain. The difference was that in the USA they had kept it up through a good, but modest, organization and a roll of people who signed the volunteer declaration.

The Student Volunteer Missionary Union

In 1891 Wilder came to Britain on his way to missionary service in India. At the Keswick Convention he was given 13 minutes in which to speak. He closed amid shouts of 'Go on! Go on!' and was besieged by students. He made a marked impression on the CICCU president and secretary and other CICCU leaders (Keswick was then nearly always well attended by CICCU men). He also touched student leaders from other places.[25] Donald Fraser from Glasgow had been converted from virtual agnosticism at the start of the Keswick week and was now called to the mission field through Wilder's speech. The CICCU men invited Wilder to Cambridge in 1892, when he spent a week there and spoke with great power. He launched the use of the SVM declaration, which was accepted after considerable hesitation. Other Keswick contacts had arranged for him to visit Aberdeen, Glasgow and Edinburgh and he was well received everywhere. His message was one of entire consecration, evangelistic and missionary zeal and the necessity of the work of the Holy Spirit if anyone were to become like Christ.

Fifty-four Cambridge students wrote to the CMS following Wilder's visit. A Cambridge man, Louis Byrde, agreed to become secretary of a national 'Student Volunteer Missionary Union' and to try to promote it outside Cambridge. Both Wilder and the Cambridge men had a national movement in mind from the start. It absorbed several other older student missionary groups, notably one in London. Byrde's room in Corpus Christi College became an astonishing hive of activity, with correspondence coming in from all over Britain. Two thousand letters are still preserved. Byrde was also a great man of prayer, with a contraption of string and weights to remove his bedclothes and so get him out of bed at 6am each morning for prayer and Bible study. A. T. Polhill-Turner was back on leave from China and became the first travelling secretary for one year. But the Union was to be essentially a 'student to student' affair.

A conference was arranged in 1893 at Keswick for a week preceding the convention and students from a number of other universities were present. From 9 to 11 each morning the time was taken up with SVMU business, but 11.30am to 1pm was used to discuss the advancement of Christian Unions in the universities of the British Isles. Missionary zeal did not neglect the home field and the leaders of the SVMU were also leaders of the growing fellowship of university CUs. The SVMU travelling secretary was the one person to visit extensively for the Christian student cause.

They immediately began to plan for an Inter-University Christian Union and in 1894 adopted the name 'British Colleges Christian Union'. The SVMU travelling secretary reported SVMU groups in sixty colleges and with 700 members. 'We are', he reported, 'in the midst of the largest, most influential and most permanent missionary revival that Great Britain has ever seen.' The second SVMU travelling secretary was Donald Fraser of Glasgow. He quickly realized the need of strong CUs if there were to be a supply of men and women for the mission field. SVMU must depend on a healthy BCCU. A joint conference for the two Unions was arranged before the 1895 Keswick Convention and a joint general secretary of the SVMU and BCCU was appointed (another Cambridge man). That same year the BCCU acquired a travelling secretary of its own when Donald Fraser transferred from the SVMU to the BCCU.

The following year (1896) a large-scale missionary conference was held in Liverpool. It was called the International Student Missionary Conference and was the first public event in the life of the movement. Speakers included C. T. Studd and G. L. Pilkington of Uganda ('Pilks'), who were home on leave. Over 500 men and 120 women were present and the excitement of the gathering gave a new vision. It was decided to adopt the 'Watchword' ('The evangelization of the world in this generation'). A group was set up to take the Watchword to the churches and get them to adopt it officially. Douglas Thornton and G. T. Manley (both hot from the CICCU) were sent to the Archbishop of Canterbury. The Watchword became a major factor in a growing worldwide missionary movement. Delegates were sent to the USA conference.

In 1895 the SVMU movement worldwide had led to the founding of the World Student Christian Federation, and in 1898 the BCCU began to call itself 'the Student Movement', which was the name of their new magazine. It was not until 1905 that the movement officially changed its name to the Student Christian Movement.

If this sounds a somewhat breathless series of developments, the answer must be that it was. Once the movement existed at grass roots and Robert Wilder had lit the touch-paper, it took only five years to grow into a national movement of both foreign and home evangelistic zeal. Wilder played a significant part in starting the international WSCF.

Douglas Thornton

The very speed of the process, however, had its dangers. Douglas Thornton was a firebrand whose enthusiasm recognized no obstacles. He had been an outstanding leader in Cambridge, and wherever he went he took a fishing-rod which was used, when attached to an alarm clock, to remove his bedclothes early in the morning. He was consumed with zeal for spiritual life and for the spread of the gospel. By 1895, however, attempts had been made to get speakers who were far from evangelical to address the conferences and Thornton saw no danger in this. In the event, none of those speakers could come and the movement remained firmly in evangelical hands for the time being. But the zeal for missionary recruitment and the aim of evangelizing the world 'in this generation' drove some of the leaders to brush aside theological considerations if only more men and women could be persuaded to volunteer for overseas service.

The Liverpool conference was a turning point. From

being a largely unnoticed, grass-roots, student movement the SCM and the Volunteer Movement became known to church leaders. The leaders of SCM also turned their attention to cultivating the interest of church leaders, including many who were not evangelicals. In his zeal to reach everyone Thornton not only succeeded in interesting the Bishop of London but did much to draw into the movement the non-evangelical theological colleges. He worked tirelessly for a Conference of Theological Students at which the Watchword could be put before them, and in 1898 it was held with 169 students and twenty-four theological college staff. Most of the Free Church colleges were represented, but very few of the Anglican ones.

It was here that the movement met a hitherto unseen problem. Thornton had proposed that, as a demonstration of their fundamental unity, the Nicene Creed should be recited together by the whole conference and a card had been printed for this purpose. Some of the students protested vigorously because they 'were not convinced of all the truth that it embodied', and the proposal was dropped. Thornton commented afterwards that he believed that 'no one who has let the spirit of the Watchword dominate his thought and life' (one wishes that he had said 'the spirit of the gospel' or 'the spirit of the cross of Christ') could fail in the end to come to 'nearer visions of the truth in Christ'. He believed that the missionary vision that fired the movement would lead men back to unity *in the faith*. He saw that 'we cannot go and teach to men the opposites of truth'; but he was an optimist and was proved wrong. Evangelistic zeal does not necessarily lead to biblical orthodoxy.

In 1898 the SVMU, the BCCU and the new Theological Colleges Department were merged to form one movement at the insistence of Thornton. This was against the strong arguments of the more cautious and discerning G. T. Manley, who was then a fellow of Christ's College. Manley feared that the merger would alter the SVMU and the CUs and lead them to lose their distinctiveness. Manley, who was probably the ablest-minded leader in the movement, felt so strongly on the matter that, when outvoted, he resigned. In the long run his fears proved to be well founded.

The Student Christian Movement

The century ended with a new situation. The SCM had become a recognized movement of importance. It was no longer student led in the same way as it had been ten years earlier. The powerful leaders were young graduates – several of them from Cambridge. But they were moving into ecclesiastical politics, where pure enthusiasm was not enough, and they were easily at a loss. Their superb vision and evangelistic and missionary zeal provided inadequate safeguards. Just when the leaders thought that the movement was strong and growing so fast that it could carry all before it, the seeds of future disaster were being sown. They were overconfident and insufficiently self-critical. Numbers seemed all important if the world were to be evangelized in that generation. They could not believe that truth needed defence as well as proclamation, and in any case they were set on going abroad themselves and would have to leave the leadership to others. They believed that the missionary spirit would bring doctrinal agreement as it had, in measure, helped to bring new life.

There was also a growing link with the World Student Christian Federation. Delegates went to WSCF Conferences and WSCF leaders, particularly John R. Mott from the USA, frequently visited Britain. He was the main missioner for the CICCU in 1896, 1898, 1905 and 1908.[26] This gave a new vision, not only for evangelism worldwide, but for a worldwide church with its own indigenous leadership. It was a thrilling and to most people a totally new perspective. To some it became an excuse for a sort of religious eclecticism – let every man have his own view without mutual criticism. A division began to appear within the ranks of the movement's leadership – and the leadership was evangelical almost to a man. Some, like Wilder, Manley and most of the CICCU leaders, remained robustly biblical and were drawn increasingly into defending the truth as they saw it. Others, like Thornton and Mott, while not changing their own position, were so anxious to bring in everyone that they refused to contend for an evangelical position so long as everyone was zealous.

These dangers were as yet discerned by only a few. The SVMU had enormous momentum and it was difficult to stand back and be critical when caught up in such a remarkable movement of zeal for the gospel and self-sacrificing service. By 1933, 3,600 members of the SVMU had actually gone abroad with British missionary societies and the number for the SVM in America was far larger. It was probably the greatest missionary movement among students that the world has seen. Most Christian students were having to face up to the possibility that they were called by God to go overseas, and in those days overseas service was not only professional suicide; it was dangerous to life and health in most parts of the world. A great many of the CICCU leaders joined SVMU, though by no means all actually went overseas.

The life of CICCU members

It is possible to reconstruct to some extent the life of the CICCU men of the late 1890s. At the time of the CICCU's centenary some who were in these groups were still living, and a decade before that there were plenty of them to talk to. It was a day of close and lasting friendships – not, of course, between men and women, but within the company of each sex. Most CICCU members spent a good deal of time in a warm circle of four to ten close friends, and a larger circle of those they met at the DPM and on vacation missions, etc. They visited one another's homes, spent holidays together and not infrequently married one another's sisters. These friendships held for a lifetime and were enormously significant after Cambridge as people scattered into the world of the ministry, missionary work or the professions. These groups were perhaps sometimes too defensive, but they were frank and genuine. The college groups and the Missionary Bands were often a focus. There was considerable outreach to others who were friends from sport and work. The Keswick influence was beginning to have the effect of making groups a little too inward-looking.

We have to remember that most students were not sceptics, however. They usually believed in a general way in the truth of Christianity. When students spoke of their faith coming alive or of a new experience of consecration it was often what we would describe as conversion or coming to a personal faith, not necessarily involving a dramatic change of life. Many, like Douglas Thornton and Theodore Woods, who came from evangelical homes, did not get going spiritually until they had a fresh experience at Cambridge or Keswick, often in their first year. Such 'newly awakened' Christians would drop their gambling and their heavy drinking, if those had been their custom. Their aim in life and their use of time and money would change; but they still had – as students usually do – plenty of natural points of contact with many non-Christians. Their cultural background was similarly religious and many of their common interests, such as sport, music, practical jokes and perhaps shooting and walking, were shared.

Sport was particularly important and many CICCU

men were prominent in cricket and rowing. Bicycling – sometimes tandem – was a new amusement. It was a CICCU man and his friend on a tandem who tried to break a record by riding 100 miles without a stop and were dismounted by a humpback bridge after ninety-nine miles. Many students walked for a couple of hours in the afternoon for exercise and pleasure. On Sundays they were often busy with Sunday schools or Open-airs, and speaking in the Open-airs was for many a kind of crossing of the Rubicon. Once they had done that they began to speak to their friends.

Personal devotions were very important. The Morning Watch was constantly emphasized and practised.[27] Prayer was very important and informal corporate prayer in small groups was the norm. Small, purely social, tea parties often ended in prayer together and the DPM was a focus and a school of prayer. Personal evangelism and persistent prayer for the conversion or spiritual blessing of friends were expected; taking friends to the Sunday evening evangelistic meeting or to the Keswick Conference was the accepted climax of it.

The rise of the Children's Special Service Mission and Scripture Union was an important factor. It was not only the encouragement of personal daily Bible study that helped, but the involvement with holiday seaside missions and camps. These were an enormous encouragement and many young converts were taken off immediately to beach missions with a Cambridge team and there pushed into public witness for the first time. A sense of spiritual responsibility for the boys who had been in your tent in the summer camp was a school of pastoral and evangelistic training for which many lived to be grateful, and it had in its turn an effect on evangelism in the university. Because a simple gospel message was seen to transform lives in the vacation, students came back with fresh confidence in the power of the gospel – but sometimes also with the feeling that fellow students should be evangelized just as if they were schoolboys. Over the years the CICCU has owed an enormous debt to this work (and vice versa), but has sometimes been over-influenced by the thrill of children's evangelism towards neglecting depth and critical thought.

Indeed, it must be said that theological depth was not a notable feature of the CICCU in this period. In all subjects plenty of members got first-class degrees, but as a rule study was directed more to missionary study than to theology or apologetics, apart of course from the straightforward study of the Bible. Louis Byrde, for instance, was described as follows: 'He was neither a thinker nor to any extent a reader; he was, however, a painstaking and regular Bible student, a man of prayer and a man of action.'[28] He became a first-class missionary.

During the Boer War, when Lord Kitchener was given an honorary degree in 1898, and again when the siege of Mafeking was relieved in 1900, the university went wild; shutters were torn off shopfronts and wooden railings lifted from gardens and from the Backs for a huge bonfire in the market place. But, being gentlemen, at least one CICCU member remembered going round the shops next day to offer to pay for the damage. Student pranks could be more destructive and dangerous than they were later and conflict between the 'town' and the 'gown' was still in evidence (it had been intense fifty years before). Cambridge was also an intensely male community. When in 1897 the Senate was voting on the question of admitting members of the women's colleges to titular degrees (i.e. allowing them to put BA after their name if they passed their exams), Trinity Street was festooned with effigies of women and Caius had a banner 'Get you to Girton, Beatrice, get you to Newnham, here is no place for maids.' But life was leisurely. Horse trams were instituted in 1880 to take people to and from the station. Reputedly slower than walking, they continued until 1914. Horse buses traversed the town from 1896.

Some CICCU leaders later lamented that they were so involved in the CICCU that they had little time to benefit from the cultural and intellectual riches of student life. But often they made these criticisms from a position of great responsibility in the church or the professions, which suggests that their CICCU involvement had in fact taught them some very important lessons. It had given them a disciplined use of time which stood them in better stead than the often lazy enjoyment of culture and society that was the attitude of most of their peers. It would have been good to do both; but if there were not time for both, it is not at all clear that they suffered any loss through choosing what they did.[29]

Chapter 4
1900–10
The battle for the truth

By 1900 the British Student Christian Movement seemed from the outside to be set for a period of steady growth in size and influence. Many within the movement, however, were aware of a growing tension. On the one hand the heirs of the evangelical tradition, epitomized by the CICCU as the oldest and largest Christian Union, remained unchanged in their evangelistic, missionary, Bible exposition and devotional emphases. On the other hand there were those who increasingly clearly did not want the movement to be narrowly evangelical. Most of them – perhaps all – had an evangelical background. But they were increasingly friendly to the new liberalism of continental theology, and already by 1901 many of the SCM leaders were committed to a liberal-critical approach to the Bible. The SCM general secretary, Tissington Tatlow, called it 'the modern view of the Bible' and described it later as 'The great movement of the Spirit manifested in . . . Higher Criticism.'[30]

Theological liberalism

The issues were not all clear cut. A more *scholarly* approach to the exposition of the Bible was, in itself, good, and the older evangelicals were often too superficial. But along with this a *rationalistic* approach came in, and was welcomed. People began to argue that we should acknowledge only those parts of the Bible that are intellectually acceptable. This was resisted by the evangelicals, more by instinct than by theological acumen, and they were therefore often driven by reaction into a slightly anti-intellectual stance. If scholarship led to such an abandonment of biblical truths, then they were against all scholarship.

Often the new rationalistic approach meant accepting clever but highly speculative reconstructions of the Bible that appealed to the current evolutionary philosophy of religion. Anything in the Bible that did not fit in with such a scheme was deemed to be an error. The classical expression of this view appeared in such phrases as 'It is incredible that . . .', 'We cannot nowadays believe that . . .' Wellhausen's influential *History of Israel and Judah*, which had this fundamental approach but put it over with great skill, was first published in the *Encyclopaedia Britannica* in 1881 (article 'Israel') and also as a book in 1885.[31] The rationalistic (not rational) principle meant that all revealed truth was to be accepted only if it could be justified at the bar of reason. Because many had a strong orthodox background the first effect of this was not to throw everyone into wholesale doubt, but quietly to destroy all revealed authority.

Christian truths were now spoken of from the pulpit as 'I think . . .', 'It seems to me that . . .', 'I believe . . .', 'I suppose we would all agree . . .' The element of authority expressed in the words 'Thus says the Lord' became inappropriate. The Bible was used now to illustrate truths accepted on rational grounds, not to prove truth. Evangelicals felt the hurt most because they had relied on Bible preaching, and they reacted most sharply against it. That is to say, those who were not intellectually overwhelmed by the tide of thought reacted; sometimes they overreacted into a rather negative attitude to all theology and all intellectual activity. But they were right in seeing that the question at issue was absolutely fundamental: Has God spoken?

Apologetics

Along with this went the question of the place that should be given to apologetics. All were concerned to answer the new sceptical spirit. Scientific materialism was beginning to be influential. Many students were doubting the basic elements of Christian faith that had been taken for granted by the majority twenty years earlier, even by those who were not personal believers at all. These doubts also affected CU members. It has to be admitted that the more liberal elements in the SCM and in the CICCU – apart from G. T. Manley and a few others – were the most eager to deal with such problems. Evangelicals tended to answer with a fresh assertion of the truth; the more liberal leaders came down to sit where the doubters sat and often tried harder than others to understand and then to answer them. But because they no longer held strongly to the sufficiency and reliability of the biblical revelation, they tended to give away too much in order to keep the doubters within the movement. Apologetics has always been a dangerous occupation and this generation fell into the standard traps without realizing it. A profound optimism about human nature was accepted and made them unwary of the dangers for themselves or their hearers of not keeping close to revealed truth. They felt sure that everyone would come back to the truth in the end, because they were so good-hearted.

For a long time people of these two traditions worked together in the CICCU and the SCM. The polarization happened only gradually, but it was made inevitable by the SCM's commitment to rationalistic higher criticism of the Bible. By 1901 that position was accepted by many SCM leaders and by 1906 this was open and more or less official; but even in 1900 some leaders saw the nature of the coming conflict.

Causes of weakness

The evangelicals of the older school tended to tackle all problems by direct biblical preaching. The Keswick devotional emphasis and concern about sanctification and a personal experience of the work of the Holy Spirit held the major place in their programme. To such people the academic theological debates about the Bible seemed unprofitable.

At a crucial stage they also lost some of their more scholarly leaders from the student scene. Handley Moule, who was a model of accurate exposition and had enormous influence in Cambridge, became Bishop of Durham in 1901. He was then largely taken up with diocesan affairs for which he was not specially gifted. In any case he was no longer in Cambridge and he was not replaced by anyone of like calibre. In Oxford F. J. Chavasse, who was in many ways a similar leader to Moule, accepted the bishopric of Liverpool in 1900. Both had run crowded weekly Greek Testament expositions and had helped many to care for conservative and scholarly handling of the sacred text in a truly devotional and, at the same time, biblically and theologically accurate way. Moule's dictum 'There should be no such thing as undevotional theology or untheological devotion' was an ideal that few others followed.

The younger 'intellectuals' tended to expound the Bible less and tried instead to grapple with 'problems'. Speakers tended to be either devotional *or* theological, and if theological to be commonly influenced by rationalistic liberalism. If Moule and Chavasse had stayed on in Cambridge and in Oxford respectively for fifty-four years as Simeon had done, the history might have been very different.

Another factor was that many of the best leaders, including some of the most shrewd thinkers, went abroad as missionaries. Douglas Thornton had left for Egypt by 1898 and died of typhoid in 1908. Pilkington had died in Uganda in 1898. G. T. Manley and Robert Wilder were in India and in those days could not even be adequately consulted. When these missionary leaders came back to speak in CUs and at conferences, they were inspiring and challenging, but no longer in close touch with what was going on.

Those who were left to run the SCM and the World Student Christian Federation were not all so clear headed theologically, although they retained their evangelistic zeal and emphasis on prayer. A historian has recently affirmed that one of the main reasons for the decline of 'the evangelical party' in the Church of England in the latter part of the nineteenth century was that their best minds were buried (either literally or metaphorically) in the malarial swamps of Africa, leaving theological teaching and leadership to anyone else who liked to take it on.[32] And, of course, missionary casualties were high. The cause (let alone the cure) of malaria was discovered only in 1895. The average life of the bishops of Sierra Leone was at one stage not much more than two years. This missionary bloodletting was their glory and the foundation of evangelical churches all round the world. Indeed, without the missionary zeal there would have been relatively little evangelical blood in the veins. It need not, and should not, have led to weakness at home. But evangelical leadership was nearly overwhelmed in the events of the next fifteen years.

One reason for this was the lack of a sufficient group of the best men giving their attention to theological training and biblical theologizing.

It is possible for us, with the wisdom of hindsight, to see some of the things that went wrong. But we must confess that we could easily have made the same mistakes and that we must learn from the past. Liberalism seemed to be a way of making Christianity more acceptable and relevant to the new scientific generation. Most of those who went liberal did so believing that they had to move from the old position because of modern discoveries. They also believed that the shift would enable them to win over those who were abandoning faith because of the sceptical and rationalistic spirit of the age. As has often happened before, they absorbed the ideas they set out to combat. The leaders of this movement themselves became rationalistic in order, so they thought, to combat rationalism.

The SCM was progressively taken over by liberal theology so that evangelicals found it impossible to maintain their position within it. In fact, apart from the CICCU and isolated individuals, the whole student movement including the High Church section was overwhelmingly swept into the liberal net. It was soon possible for people to argue that anyone holding to traditional orthodoxy was simply not an educated person.

The inclusive principle

The trouble for the student world started with inclusiveness. The Watchword of the SVMU, which was not after all a biblical idea in itself, pushed people to take risks for the sake of numbers. If the gospel were to be preached seriously throughout the world in that generation, then the *number* of missionaries seemed to be all-important. Membership of SVMU was carefully watched and advertised. Everyone began to care too much about the size and influence of the movement. To be caught up with 'the spirit of the Watchword', to use Thornton's phrase, became for some a sort of special 'experience' that reduced critical thought and brushed aside all opposition. It did not induce in most people a renewed concern for the content of the gospel.

The involvement with the theological colleges, where continental liberalism had become influential, brought what Tatlow called 'the modern view of the Bible' on to the SCM platform. A great effort was made to get the High Church colleges, the 'High Church Party' and 'Broad Church Party' leaders to take an interest in the Watchword and later in the movement.[33] The attempt to get the churches to adopt the Watchword failed, partly because most of the Church of England leadership was not evangelical and suspected anything from that source. Tatlow, and Mott on his frequent visits to Britain, realized this and therefore worked hard to get the archbishops and other official leaders interested and to broaden the theological base of SCM to make it more widely acceptable. In order to do so they asked non-evangelicals to speak at the conferences.

By 1900 controversy was beginning about speakers. In 1903 G. T. Manley and three other missionaries home on furlough asked the leaders to restore the evangelical emphasis at the conferences. In 1904 another group of senior friends, including E. S. Woods, wrote similarly. Canon Webb-Peploe, a leading evangelical minister, wrote to the secretary expressing doubts about appearing on the conference programme as an alternative speaker to men of other outlook. The office of the SCM was bombarded from all sides asking them to have more evangelicals, more High Churchmen or more liberals, according to the standpoint of the writer. It was quickly accepted, however, that the movement was theologically inclusive and that evangelicals could no longer expect to dominate it, let alone have the platform to themselves as they had done ten years before.

The sequence of events, or rather trends, was not a simple one. The different factors interlocked. The attempt to be inclusive of the High Church party broke the evangelical dominance and started a *self-conscious* inclusivist policy. The High Church leaders who were willing to come in, however, were not usually liberal at the beginning. Theological liberalism slipped in, almost unnoticed at first, from the theological colleges. It was only when the inclusivist principle was accepted and acknowledged that the presence of liberal speakers was defended on the same grounds as the presence of High Churchmen.

In 1910 the SCM general secretary, Tissington Tatlow, wrote to a protesting London medical student, 'It is part of the Student Movement position that the movement, as such, does not determine what is orthodox and what is unorthodox. We must live off the life of the Christian bodies which are composing the movement ... I do not know of any teacher of the Bible who commands a wider following among theological students at present than Dr Peake (of *Peake's Commentary*, a Primitive Methodist who caused the protest by his talk at a summer conference) ... his views on the Bible are those that are taught in almost every theological college in the British Isles.'[34]

At first Eugene Stock, the highly influential editorial secretary of the CMS, was anxious about what was happening, but Tatlow managed to persuade him that all was well. The CMS was concerned because so many of their missionaries came from the CICCU, but Stock and others in CMS did not see that the rift had far wider implications.[35]

Contrasting stances

The point must be made that it was only very gradually that the different views crystallized into contrasting 'stances' like this. The letter quoted above, however, shows how things were moving in the SCM and where they ended up by 1910. By that date there was a deliberate refusal to hold to any particular theological position and an equally deliberate agreement to give prominence to whatever was prominent in the churches. By the same date many of the orthodox evangelicals realized that they must stand clearly and unequivocally for biblical orthodoxy and that this meant going in a different direction from the national SCM and the worldwide WSCF.

One other change turned out to be of major importance. In 1897 the SCM conference had been moved from Keswick, partly in order that speakers of other theological outlooks would be more likely to come.[36] It was rightly felt that Keswick, with its strongly evangelical tradition, would discourage some from speaking. This greatly reduced the Cambridge attendance at SCM conferences. Most Cambridge men still went to the Keswick Convention and perhaps also to the joint CICCU/OICCU conference. Not so many came to the SCM summer conferences at Curbar, Matlock, Baslow, etc. (and finally, from 1912, at The Hayes, Swanwick, which was acquired primarily for the SCM).

CICCU and SCM

The result of all this was that the CICCU avoided being drawn into the growing eclecticism of the SCM. Some of its leaders were involved and were influenced that way, but they were few. It so happened that there were not so many CICCU men in the SCM leadership at this time, although there were several leading OICCU members. The very influential secretary of the SCM, Tissington Tatlow, was a Dublin man who did not understand Cambridge and became increasingly an ecclesiastical politician. He was not the first nor the last evangelical to have lost his critical faculties under flattery and in the company of those who were counted great in the churches. In his official history of the SCM he repeatedly confessed that the initiatives were going more and more to senior friends of the movement rather than to the students. He also revealed how important it was for him to talk with prominent church leaders. Some of these friends, such as Bishop Charles Gore, had never been in a CU and some who had were no longer of the same spirit or doctrine because they had been absorbing liberal theology.

By 1905 there was not only conflict within the SCM, but particular tension between the student-led CICCU, which was still the Cambridge branch of the SCM, and the SCM national leadership. At the grass-roots level all over the country many students came up from evangelical churches and homes, but they had little power outside Cambridge. A doctor at King's College Hospital, London, wrote of the wishes of a London Medical Students Committee, 'The Committee want more of the "old stuff", they want more of the younger speakers – people with the cutting edge still left on, even if it is a bit jaggy. A good many keen people of the evangelical way have said to me lately that they had taken younger friends to Baslow (the SCM summer conference) to get conversion hot; but the friends hadn't had it, so "next year I'm going to Keswick". I've heard that a good many times and it makes me rather sad . . . I think the committee's aspirations are summed up in the idea of more Robert Wilder theology' (Robert Wilder came on to the British SCM staff from 1906 until 1915). The same letter also says, 'I am not so sure that we ought to address our Mother the Movement

quite so haughtily.'[37] Mother SCM was evidently beginning to be above criticism.[38]

Between 1905 and 1910 the conflict between the
CICCU and the national SCM became more explicit.
They were not only pulling in different directions, but
were beginning to doubt whether they could continue to
work together. The CICCU was strong. In 1903 there had
been an outstanding Mission with Prebendary Webb-
Peploe leading. Comparisons were made with the Moody
Mission of 1882 and, as in that Mission, not only were
many non-Christians converted, but many Christians were
greatly helped. It was straight, hot, biblical preaching. The
first sermon was on 'the wages of sin is death; but the gift
of God is eternal life through Jesus Christ our Lord'.
Webb-Peploe was over sixty and represented the older
evangelicals, but had remarkable ability to reach students.
He held a short after-meeting each night and then invited
men to stand to confess their new-found faith. He encouraged them to be bold and to put a memorial card, indicat-
ing their profession, on display in their rooms. The DPM
took on a new lease of life and a year later the principal of
Ridley Hall spoke of 'a great wave of blessing which has
come upon us'. Many Christians learnt to take a definite
stand.

Evangelism in and out of term-time

CICCU members were still much involved in the SVMU,
even if they played little part in the other sections of the
SCM. In 1904, for instance, twenty-six Cambridge men
went on one of the SVMU missionary campaigns in
Huddersfield, where the aim was to win volunteers for the
mission field from the churches. They also had fresh interests of their own. They already had the Sunday school and
open-air preaching in the suburbs and villages around
Cambridge and the involvement with the CSSM

(now Scripture Union) in the summer; they then started the Cambridge University Mission in Bermondsey. There were at that time a good many 'settlements' and missions, run often by High Church groups, but this Mission provided both a boys' club and a dispensary. It also gave priority to direct evangelistic work in a way that was true of few of the others. For the next sixty years it also provided a field of vacation service that was a help to those many CICCU men who took part, and a means of reaching totally unchurched young men from a slum area. An impressive number of future ministers, teachers and missionaries (including at least one missionary bishop) were very poor boys from Bermondsey reached through the CUM.

The year 1905 saw a remarkable evangelistic weekend with the American evangelist Charles Alexander; and then, in the same year, another Mission led by Dr John R. Mott. Mott was by then the chief moving spirit of the WSCF and a powerful force in the British SCM. Dr Mott was an evangelical and a good student evangelist. His own theological position never changed explicitly, but as he got older he became less decisive and definite. Robert Wilder, on the other hand, who had first brought Mott into the work, remained a staunch evangelical with a clear and incisive biblical ministry.

By that stage Mott could not see the importance of keeping the movement solidly evangelical. A deputation from the CICCU called on him and begged him to use his influence in the WSCF to preserve its evangelical heritage. Mott could not see the point. Indeed, it seems that privately he was definitely against this policy. He was already set on an inclusivist course and seemed to see its success around the world in the growing number of students in the WSCF. He continued to push the British SCM in that direction and his own overwhelming personal influence was hard to resist. In Cambridge he was still accepted as an evangelist and at that stage at least did not alter the pattern of CICCU activity.

'The majority of the devoutly Christian young men in Cambridge are probably evangelical in their views' was a contemporary comment in the *Church Quarterly Review*. High Church influence was weak in Cambridge, whereas Oxford was its focus. A growing group of senior men were willing to speak for the CICCU, though many of them were not of the same theological outlook. Montagu Butler, the Master of Trinity College, had been helped in the CU as an undergraduate and loved to expound the Bible, but he would not preach on the atonement because he did not really understand it. He too had been a teacher at 'Jesus Lane', but he must have been something of an exception to the staunch orthodoxy of the majority of that group. R. H. Kennett, the Professor of Hebrew, was becoming increasingly clearly a liberal in his view of the Bible and later his view of the atonement, but he was also willing to speak for the CICCU. The CICCU was accustomed to senior help and appreciated it and accepted these men as speakers without much criticism. But there were no senior men of a strongly evangelical orthodoxy to take the place of Handley Moule and the several science professors who had helped during the Moody Mission and the Cambridge Seven period.

Deepening division

At the same time a growing group of young university teachers became critical of the CICCU's narrowness and tried to persuade the leaders to broaden out. After a while, they began to discuss the possibility of creating a new SCM branch in Cambridge which would enable them to get more speakers of other points of view on to the platform. In Cambridge itself, the senior pressure was all for an inclusivist policy. Webb-Peploe, most of the regular

CICCU speakers and friends in other parts of the country repeatedly urged them to stand firm. Ridley Hall was going somewhat liberal and Holy Trinity and the other churches were not a strong influence either way.

In 1905 a number of seniors took a separate initiative and invited Father Ball of the Community of the Resurrection (strongly High Church) to lead an independent Mission in Great St Mary's Church. The CICCU was invited to support. It was said that Ball believed in conversion and would preach for it, and the CICCU was at first inclined to agree. They had never faced this sort of cooperation problem before and had little experience to guide them. The matter was settled, however, when G. T. Manley (who was home again from the mission field) gave the weekend Bible Reading on justification by faith. Issues at stake were spelt out and the CICCU decided not to support the Mission. They were publicly criticized for this by the Bishop of London and others, but when the Mission actually took place, most of the evangelicals realized that the decision had been right. The missioner did not mean the same thing as they did by conversion or the means of entering and growing in the Christian life.

In 1905 also, at the last of the series of twenty-eight joint CICCU/OICCU conferences, the OICCU shocked their Cambridge counterparts by suggesting that the CUs be broadened to enable Unitarians to accept membership. This was the inclusivist principle gone mad and was even contrary to the SCM policy of the day, but it made the CICCU realize what was the direction of the policies outside Cambridge.

Reform?

In 1907, 1908 and 1909 the CICCU presidents were actively involved in the SCM central activities and were all asked to help to bring the CICCU into line. These three 'reforming presidents' in turn became enthusiastic for that task. But they could not carry the CU leadership or membership with them. It remained staunchly evangelical and preferred to maintain its own style and programme.

It is significant that, with all these pressures, the CICCU refused to lose its evangelical identity. How did they manage to stand firm when the OICCU and other CUs did not (with the partial exception of the London medical schools)? The answer must be that the biggest factor was that they were men steeped in the Bible. They read and studied the Bible avidly. They had also been careful to invite as speakers only those who would faithfully expound Scripture, and they made sure that their programme provided a healthy biblical diet.

The SCM always suspected that it was the pressure of the CICCU's senior friends that held them. Such friends did urge loyalty to 'the old paths', but they had less opportunity of influence than the concerted efforts of senior men in Cambridge, the succession of three 'reforming' presidents in a row and the arguments of nearly all the national SCM leaders. By the grace of God the CICCU members stood firm for a witness to biblical orthodoxy because they were constantly exposed to the Bible at both a personal and a corporate level.

It has repeatedly happened in the history of evangelical movements that those outside them have attributed their stubbornness and consistency to some outside influence. That is almost the only explanation available to those who do not believe that, if people keep on reading the Bible in a humble and teachable spirit, they keep on coming independently to the same conclusions. It is sincerely believed by those outside that there must have been some such overwhelming power to prevent the CICCU following a broader and looser policy. But the college reps and the vast majority of the members were solidly evangelical. They studied the Bible daily for themselves and in informal groups and the weekend Bible Readings and sermons gave them consistent biblical theology. The reforming presidents could not swing the general body of the student members.

Partly because the CICCU was so solidly biblical, people who held strongly to other outlooks did not join it in large numbers. In 1906 some of those dissatisfied with the CICCU formed a new religious society, the Cambridge University Church Society. It was broadly Church of England and its published aim was 'to promote and consolidate the work of the Church of England in Cambridge'. It grew rapidly to a membership of 600 – far larger than the CICCU. A Nonconformist Union was also created about that time. The CICCU was therefore no longer the sole student religious society and not even the largest, though its active membership was probably comparable to that of the others. The creation of these societies also had the effect that some enthusiastic Christians of other traditions did not attempt to influence the CICCU from within, though there was an overlap of membership with the other societies. In other universities, where the CU was the only major religious body, the pressure to broaden out often became stronger because there was nothing else for people to join. Unless a CU stood very firm, as the CICCU did, a process of gradual dilution was hard to avoid. If they stood firm, other societies were likely to arise in the highly religious world of a place like Cambridge. But nowhere else were they firm enough to avoid progressive compromise of what had been a stoutly biblical tradition.

Three possibilities

Broadly speaking, three possibilities presented themselves to the CICCU. The first was that the CICCU should enter into some sort of federal union with the Church Society and the Nonconformist Union. The second was that the CICCU should come into line with the rest of the SCM and broaden its basis and platform. It soon became clear that, if this happened, a significant section of the CICCU would probably leave and form a new CU. The third was that the CICCU should disaffiliate from the SCM and leave the SCM free to start its own new branch in Cambridge with the enthusiastic backing of a considerable group of seniors.

In 1908 experiments were carried out in the direction of the first solution. Dr John R. Mott came up for his fourth and last CICCU Mission.[39] This time, however, it was jointly sponsored by a council drawn from all the religious societies. The first of the reforming presidents, R. L. Pelly, was enthusiastic about this policy. Outwardly this was an extremely successful Mission. It had superb publicity. The Bishops of London and Ely signed a message commending the Mission. The Guildhall was filled every night and Mott had an after-meeting each time and on the last night asked men to stand, signifying their response. He commented, 'After each evangelistic appeal a large number of men accepted Christ.' Mott's appeal had perhaps shifted a little from his earlier 'to accept Christ as their personal Saviour' to a new emphasis on 'to follow Jesus Christ'. But there was no repudiation of his evangelical emphases. One hundred and fifty gave in their names in token of decision. It was said that 'over three hundred men decided for Christ as a result of the campaign'.

The results, however, were disappointing. The follow-up was thorough and the CICCU's public reputation had probably never been higher, but few of the converts stood firm. Gradually lethargy set in and DPM attendance fell very low. Bellerby, the third reforming president, became convinced that the remedy was to broaden the platform even further, drop the Open-airs and perhaps drop the DPM in favour of more formal intercessions. The preachers at Sunday services became mixed in their theology and sometimes the CICCU joined with other societies to hear famous non-evangelical preachers such as Bishop Charles Gore.

No-one of that generation had seen the CICCU in its former strength. But G. F. B. Morris, the vice-president, and a number of strongly evangelical friends became thoroughly disillusioned. They included some sons of the 1882 generation who had at least heard of greater days – Stanley Smith's son and J. E. K. Studd's son were among them. It seemed to them that the CICCU was now so uncertain in its witness that, unless it could be restored to a consistent biblical ministry, it had better be abandoned. They began to think in terms of a new body independent of the SCM, because they did not see how else to realize their vision for a clear evangelical witness again.

Tissington Tatlow, from his own account of the matter, did not treat it very seriously. His friends in SCM agreed. Tatlow had by that time taken the bit between his teeth and was heading vigorously in the direction of an increasingly inclusivist policy. He regarded the CICCU's stubborn evangelicalism as little more than a nuisance. Once it was out of the SCM, the SCM leaders expected the CICCU to wither away. Tatlow made up his mind in favour of disaffiliation. His own words are: 'I was asked by the General Committee (of SCM) to spend some time in Cambridge and decide whether it seemed wiser to advise the breaking of affiliation, or to make a further attempt to bring the CICCU into line with the student movement. I spent a great deal of time in Cambridge ... and in the end advised disaffiliation.'

The president, Bellerby, believed, however, that there was still hope and corresponded further with the SCM. Finally he decided that the question must be brought to a decision one way or the other. Tatlow was asked to come up again and address a general meeting of the CICCU, after which the matter would be put to a vote. Bellerby wrote, 'I had complete confidence that Tissington Tatlow would win the day for what I wanted – a bigger Christian Union reaching a bigger circle of men.' He hoped that the CICCU would follow the recent example of the OICCU, who had accepted the SCM's inclusive policy (though, in the event, only temporarily).

The parting of the ways

The meeting took place in March 1910. Tatlow spoke in favour of broadening the CICCU. A long discussion followed, but to Bellerby's surprise the motion was defeated and that meant disaffiliation. The CICCU general committee met soon after to make a formal decision. To quote the CICCU Secretary, 'A tremendous discussion took place, with a real fight on the part of those desiring retention of affiliation to reverse the decision of the previous vote. For a long time the issue hung in the balance.' In the end it was decided by seventeen votes to five to stand by the decision of the previous general meeting. The SCM was sent a formal notice that 'The CICCU decides to break affiliation with the SCM' in order that both sides should be free to work unhindered in Cambridge. Morris became the president, to be followed soon after by Howard Mowll who had also been through the debate. They knew what they stood for.[40]

Thus the CICCU parted company with the SCM which it had done so much to create. To the astonishment of many, over 200 men stood by the CICCU, even though they thereby broke with a World Student Christian Federation of over 150,000 members worldwide. They were regarded either as a pathetic remnant of a once great tradition now on the way to extinction or, alternatively, as a valiant band of modern reformers, representing a challenge to others to stand for the truth against all the concerted influence and wisdom of the clever and powerful leaders of the church.

On a very small scale, there were analogies with the stand of Luther. They were going back to the original tradition which had created the CICCU. They were going back to that because they believed it to be biblical. The story has echoes of Luther's assertion 'My conscience is tied to the Word of God. Here I stand, I can do no other. So help me God.' It may seem impertinent to make the comparison. No-one is suggesting that their stand was as important as that of Luther, but they were, on a small scale, in the same tradition. They did not face personal danger for their stand. They only faced looking stupid and, what is often hard to a student, appearing to be terribly old-fashioned, stuck-in-the-mud and out of touch with reality. They also faced the need to disagree sharply with personal friends and others with whom they had previously worked happily in Christian fellowship and witness.

They challenge us in our generation to be willing to take a strong stand for an unpopular and apparently hopeless cause for the sake of loyalty to God's revealed truth; and to risk friendship, reputation and the glory of being part of a successful cause because of our faith in God and his gospel. They were trying to be loyal to what they found written in the Bible, even though they were a tiny minority of educated Christians. At the time there was no glory, only an anxious testing of different possible paths; there was no certainty of success or influence on anyone else. They had only an awareness of being very much criticized by many whom they respected. They had no sense of creating history, only a conviction that they were following the path of duty.

Chapter 5
1910–20
'Not as pleasing men . . .'

Once disaffiliated from the SCM, the CICCU seemed to be hopelessly isolated. It did not see any spectacular growth or revival – in fact, its membership declined slightly. Its witness, however, was now consistent. People were being converted and built up in a biblical faith and missionary zeal increased.

After an interval the SCM founded its own branch in Cambridge and worked with a joint committee of the other existing religious societies (the Church Society, the Nonconformist Union and the very High Church Societas Trinitatis Confraternitas). Many links of friendship were maintained with the SCM. Evangelical speakers appeared with others at the SCM Conference. Robert Wilder, whose theology never wavered, was a member of the SCM staff by then, but was a welcome visitor to the CICCU on frequent occasions. R. L. Pelly, the first of the 'reforming presidents', was also on the SCM staff and clearly pulling hard in the opposite direction.[41] Many old friends regretted the breach and could not believe that it was necessary. Some criticized vigorously, but the liberal leaders in

Cambridge had the wisdom not to try to put pressure on the CICCU. They had too much respect for the duty of every man to follow his own conviction – a situation that changed considerably after the First World War.

Most observers found it acutely disappointing that a movement with the missionary tradition of the CICCU seemed to be turning its back on the opportunity of influencing the worldwide, powerful movement the SCM had become. The CICCU seemed a mere backwater. The theological colleges, and therefore the younger leadership of the churches, were rushing into liberalism without any idea of how destructive it was going to prove. They repeatedly affirmed that old-fashioned evangelicalism had no future. Most of the once-conservative High Church leaders, like Bishop Gore, had become also at least mildly liberal. They had accepted the liberal (rationalist) principle that human reason was as valid a source of our knowledge of God as the Bible and 'Tradition'. This meant in effect, of course, that they accepted only as much of the Bible and of Tradition as 'the modern mind' could find acceptable; and that proved to be less and less as time went on.

The whole Protestant world seemed to have been swept away. That some old-fashioned Church of England parishes, the Brethren, isolated Free Churches and a few students in Cambridge should hold fast was of little consequence. Even the Free Church of Scotland followed the trend. That God continued to bless the old gospel and to make strong Christians through a conservative biblical ministry was not at first so obvious as to excite comment in liberal circles.

At this distance it is also hard for us to realize how many of the fruits of a biblical upbringing most of the liberal leaders retained. They still read the Bible for themselves. Prayer was very important. Their devotional life was strong and missionary work and home evangelism attracted much self-sacrifice and zeal. The situation was far from clear cut, and it polarized only gradually. It took unusual discernment to see the difference between preaching that was fully dependent on the authoritative Word of God and preaching that used the Bible more to illustrate themes which had been arrived at on rational authority.

Many evangelical students could see little more than that the new theology omitted major emphases that they thought biblical, and even central, and that its denigration of the unique authority of the Bible was disastrous. They were not necessarily good apologists, but they were gospel-minded and knew what they and the new Christians needed and had found amid all the pressures of student life. They preached and tried to obey an authoritative Word of God. To do less was to betray their commission. They could see that the truth of the gospel was at stake.

By capturing the theological colleges, and then the SCM, theological liberalism achieved a period of domination of the church. If it had also captured the CICCU, the future of the relatively thin line of robust evangelical ministry would have been further gravely weakened. The pressures to conform were (and are) so strong in the student world that very likely it would have taken a long time before a strong strain of biblical evangelicalism would have emerged again.[42]

There were no doubt always individuals and small groups who refused to bow to the theological fashion. As it went on, the CICCU itself not only provided a steady flow of strong evangelical ministers and missionaries, but before long was making a major contribution of vision and courage to help create similar distinctively evangelical student groups all over Britain and then all round the world. Of the twenty-five members of the 1911 General Committee, for instance, twelve became missionaries, seven others were ordained at home. Of these nineteen, five became bishops. That generation in the CICCU included some who became outstanding evangelical Church of England leaders of the 1930s and 1940s at home and abroad.

Basis of Membership

Gradually the gap between the CICCU and the national SCM widened. There was considerable unhappiness with the way things were going in some of the SCM branches. They were usually still called Christian Unions and in 1910 still had the same Membership Basis as the CICCU. But the leadership was increasingly in older and definitely 'inclusivist' hands. The great idea was to produce a 'synthesis' of different traditions. Evangelical speakers became fewer at both central and local levels. Bible study outlines and similar literature produced by the SCM were increasingly boldly liberal in approach. Positive discrimination against evangelicals in certain ecumenical contexts was more frequent.[43]

Finally this drift was shown by another alteration in the SCM Basis of Membership. The old Basis of the BCCU and SCM had been 'A belief in Jesus Christ as God the Son and only Saviour of the world'. In 1902 this had been changed after long and excited debate to the CICCU Basis, 'I desire in joining this Union to declare my faith in Jesus Christ as my Saviour, my Lord and my God.' It had been a relief to discover that this provided an acceptable solution in a tussle over the rather blunt statement of the earlier Basis. At that stage those who wanted a more open Basis had been defeated.

In 1910, however, the phrase 'Jesus Christ as . . . my God' was found objectionable; after prolonged debate it was changed in 1913 to one that avoided a statement of the deity of Jesus Christ. It was argued not only that doubters should be in the movement, but that they should be voting members, lest they be discouraged.[44] Since no further statement was required of officers either, such people became increasingly influential in the SCM.

It is hard to overestimate the importance of this membership question. The clear-cut call that the CICCU Membership Basis supplied, to identify oneself as in the full sense a Christian, did much to clarify its witness over the years. It was also a challenge to generation after generation of freshers to declare that they did want to stand for their Lord in the university and acknowledge that he was their Saviour, Lord and God. It would have been easy for the CICCU to go along with the current optimism which thought that people would become orthodox once they were in the fellowship. Perhaps the very fact that the SCM went that way helped the CICCU to see how destructive of true witness that path would be. It was so clearly part of a mood of unwillingness to stand as a body for revealed truth.

Having changed the Membership Basis in this way, it was inevitable that in time the title 'Christian Union' would be felt inappropriate to an SCM branch. Tradition, however, was strong and some CUs were, after all, older than the SCM. It was not until 1929 that the title 'Christian Union' was officially abandoned by the SCM (in favour of 'SCM branch'). The older SCM groups in Oxford and elsewhere had progressively dropped 'CU' long before, so that when evangelical groups were re-formed in these universities they were usually free to adopt the old title.[45] The very idea of being a *Christian* Union, with a definite Membership Basis of the kind used by the CICCU, became a distinctive mark of the new evangelistic and evangelical groups that emerged in the next decade and began to distinguish them from SCM groups. In order to *help* non-Christians they had to be excluded from membership. It did not take long for evangelicals all round the country to realize that the CICCU had been right to make a break when it did and that otherwise it too would have lost the essentials of a clear-cut witness.

Renewed evangelism

The CICCU meanwhile was preoccupied with its own problems and opportunities. It did nothing to try to create similar groups in other universities. It abandoned the SCM summer conferences and went back to Keswick. Members spent their energies in evangelism and Bible study in Cambridge, including extensive Sunday school and Open-air work, and in the vacations were involved with the CSSM and camps. The DPM increased its attendance and the Sunday sermons reached many non-Christians. Little activity of an organized kind went on in the colleges (no college Bible Readings or prayer meetings), but the week-end speaker for the evangelistic sermon gave a Bible study at 12.30pm on Sunday as well. This Sunday Bible Reading was usually along the lines of the Keswick message of consecration and holiness and being fully yielded to God. Informal prayer among members was the rule when they met for tea and coffee.

In January 1911 it was decided to arrange another large-scale Mission and to invite the American Dr R. A. Torrey. In 1903 he had held Missions in London in which many CICCU men had assisted. Torrey usually travelled with a singer, Charles Alexander, but it was decided not to invite Alexander to Cambridge so that they should 'rely only on the power of the Word of God, without other aids to attract an audience or to lead to the conversion of souls'. Torrey came in November 1911, but there had been intense preparation – especially prayer – for nine months beforehand. Seventy members went to Keswick to prepare themselves (the membership was probably around 150).

The decision to bring Torrey aroused immediate antagonism in Cambridge. He was both an 'American revivalist' and also a scholarly and informed opponent of higher criticism. He had studied in Germany and his earlier sympathy with liberal theology had turned to determined opposition. But the CICCU asked him because he was an evangelist. There was virtually no senior support. The CICCU even had difficulty in obtaining a meeting place owing, it was believed, to senior opposition. There was a rumoured plot to kidnap Torrey on arrival. He arrived early for preparatory meetings and urged the members to do their work 'in dependence on God, on prayer, on the Word of God and the Holy Spirit, and by personal work'.

Torrey preached with logic, earnestness and spiritual power. The addresses were simple and searching. At the end of the first week many had professed conversion and stood to signify it. Torrey stayed on another week to instruct them and to give two further evangelistic addresses. A hundred Scofield Reference Bibles were given to men who had professed conversion and Torrey's emphasis on 'the Morning Watch' led, he believed, to 200 men committing themselves to spending an hour each morning in personal prayer and Bible study.

The Mission left the CICCU numerically and spiritually stronger. There were excellent speakers and crowded weekend meetings. Many of the more liberal dons, however, were offended and now regarded reunion as impossible. In particular, pressure was brought to bear on freshers in an attempt to persuade them to abandon their traditional evangelical beliefs in favour of more 'enlightened' views. Basil Atkinson, who went up in 1914, had in his first term no fewer than three ordained men (including the principal of Ridley Hall) trying to argue him out of his conservative faith.

CICCU men attended the Church Missionary Union weekly meetings as well as the activities of the SVMU in fair numbers. But even these began to raise problems. The speakers at the first became theologically mixed and the SVMU, which was part of the SCM, was very mixed in membership. In the end the CICCU men formed the Cambridge Volunteer Union for those intending missionary service, although membership overlapped with the SVMU for some time. The CVU had a membership declaration with a Bible clause in it and was much more definite than SVMU about the message to be taken to the mission field. In fact, the doctrine of Scripture and its authority lay behind the whole dispute and this became increasingly explicit as time went on. But the deity of Christ and the nature of his atonement were in the forefront of the debate most of the time.

A doctrinal statement

The CICCU began to feel the need to be more explicit about what it meant when members signed that Jesus Christ was their 'Saviour, Lord and God'. There were now more students around who could affirm this without meaning at all the same thing as the CICCU. The first step in this direction was the publication in 1913 of a booklet called *Old Paths in Perilous Times*,[46] which was always referred to in a friendly way as 'Prickly Paths'. This was a sort of apologia for the separate existence of the CICCU as a distinctive witness. It affirmed clearly that the CICCU was not going to accept any weakening on the deity of Christ, Christ's view of the Bible, the nature of the atonement or the lost state of human nature. All these truths were being doubted or challenged by Christian leaders and the booklet declared that the CICCU refused to go along with 'multilateral theology, the aggregate of many views', which had become the fashion. It was a reaffirmation of straightforward orthodox belief, with a short history of what had happened.

The 1914–18 war

Godfrey Buxton – a son of the Moody Mission convert – went up in 1913 and described how he tried to reach the fifteen men who normally sat at his table in 'Hall'. He took them to sermons and finally persuaded them to come to Keswick in July 1914 – each on a motorbike, to the terror of the villages they passed through. In August came the war, to the complete surprise of most people. The young men poured into the army and the appalling casualty lists inscribed on college war memorials contain many names of Torrey Mission converts.[47] Of Godfrey Buxton's fifteen friends, ten were killed. The university dwindled after 1915 to almost nothing. A very small group kept the DPM going for all but a short period, but that was all they could do after 1915.

The post-war generation

In 1918 wounded men began to return and tried to resume their studies. By January 1919 the university was again in full swing. The 1919 undergraduates were an extraordinary crowd. Many were very conceited. They had won the war and they almost believed that they were the heroes the popular slogans described ('a land fit for heroes to live in'). They had been through some terrible experiences, and in reaction were often careless of all restraint and serious thought. Ex-service men could do a very short course for an 'ordinary degree' which required little work. University life became rather frivolous.

A small group of CICCU men soon gathered for the DPM. Rarely more than fifteen of them at first, they were deeply in earnest. Godfrey Buxton and Norman Grubb arrived, both with military decorations for bravery and both recovering from wounds – a long process when there were no antibiotics. Buxton became president, though he was on crutches and often incapacitated. Grubb went through a spiritual experience which resulted in him giving up smoking and seeking to be, in a new sense, all out for God. The group became extremely zealous and feared no-one. They set about vigorous personal evangelism. Numbers at the DPM gradually rose to fifty.

Liberal evangelicalism

The theological scene was drastically different from that of 1914. Liberalism was rampant. Ridley Hall and Holy Trinity Church were both now representative of a new movement, 'Liberal evangelicalism'. Its leaders were often old CICCU men; but having drunk deeply of liberal theology, they were quite explicitly different in their teaching from the older evangelical tradition – much more so than the SCM leaders of 1910. The liberal evangelicals preached for decisions of a less clear kind. Their message was still centred in Jesus Christ, but their call was more vaguely to follow him and at times they were not explicit on his deity.[48] What following him meant to people depended much on their background. Of course there were gradations, but the men of the new school were so certain that they were right that the older evangelicals – now beginning to be called 'conservative evangelicals' by contrast – were to many of them a ridiculous anachronism.

E. S. Woods, the vicar of Holy Trinity, was an old CICCU man whose position had now greatly changed from his student days. He described one effect of a sermon in his church on the atonement by R. H. Kennett (the Professor of Hebrew), which must have been frankly destructive of the truth held dear by many. A faithful old Sunday school teacher came to him afterwards to offer his resignation. The 'dear old man' confessed that after that sermon he had not slept all night and the vicar commented, 'I could hardly control my amusement.' That was the problem. To both the vicar and his biographer consistent evangelicalism was simply funny in its tenacious adherence to the substitutionary death of Christ. That someone had been unable to sleep because he thought truth was in danger was comical. 'They identify Christianity with that little tiny bit of religious truth and religious experience which has come within the ken of themselves and their clique,' Woods wrote.[49] If people did not actually attack evangelical truth, as Kennett did, they regarded such truth as merely the personal fad of a few old-fashioned Christians. There might be something in it, but it was irrelevant for up-to-date people.

Nevertheless the CICCU men did not always make things easy. They attended Holy Trinity because there was nowhere better to go. During a sermon packed with literary quotations but with no Bible references, at least one CICCU man was heard muttering to himself as he thumbed through his Bible, 'I can't find these quotations anywhere in my Bible.' E. S. Woods was typical of the best kind of liberal evangelical. He was a deeply devoted and spiritually minded man. No-one doubted the reality of his experience. His warmth, humility and love were a blessing to many. But in his doctrine he had moved progressively in a liberal direction. He did not, like some others, deny the doctrines he had affirmed as a student, but he welcomed speakers who did. The content of his message became less and less explicitly biblical and therefore, from the point of view of the CICCU men, it lacked both clarity and divine authority. The Pastorate, still with two ordained men, followed the trend. Ridley Hall and most of the other traditionally evangelical churches and leaders were similar.

By contrast the CICCU men were sometimes brash, overdogmatic, and sometimes rude to their seniors in an attempt to be loyal to biblical truth. They were certainly not without their faults; but the liberal evangelicals had in their theology the seeds of their own dissolution and it was not long before their weaknesses began to emerge. The next generation of liberals did not have the same spiritual capital to draw on, having been taught differently. The CICCU had, by the grace of God, a much more biblical position and, in the long run, the power and truth of the Bible were clearly seen.

The theological lecturers were by then aggressively liberal and the college deans and chaplains had little sympathy with the CICCU. Once more its members found themselves on their own and in a position of being frankly despised, pitied or laughed at by the official religious establishment and the majority of those who mattered. If the future had been left to the churches and theological faculties, the evangelical witness would have disappeared from the university scene and, in due time, from many pulpits and congregations. Mercifully, the CICCU was not prepared to be led by the official Christian leadership any more than by the SCM leadership. Nor were they willing to be swamped by the influence of even the best of the local churches that were available.

The SCM was comparatively strong, intellectual and well supported. Some members, however, felt keenly that they lacked certain things the CICCU could supply. They did not want the CICCU's theology, but they wanted its zeal and prayer life and whole-heartedness. They could not believe that a watered-down message was the cause of their own weaknesses. To the liberal evangelicals it seemed obvious that so long as one 'can call Jesus Lord and slave for His Kingdom', no more should be needed.[50] History has proved that that was wrong – fatally wrong – and reading the New Testament had warned the CICCU of the fact.

'Of first importance'

When Norman Grubb was secretary in 1919 (he left direct for the mission field in December of that year), he and the president met a deputation from the SCM to discuss whether they could join forces. The DPM was continued all afternoon that day until the CICCU delegates returned. Grubb describes it as follows: 'After an hour's conversation which got us nowhere, one direct and vital question was put: "Does the SCM consider the atoning blood of Jesus Christ as the central point of their message?" And the answer given was, "No, not as central, although it is given a place in our teaching." That settled the matter, for we explained to them at once that the atoning blood was so much the heart of our message that we could never join with a movement which gave it a lesser place.'[51]

That the atonement was the crucial issue was significant. The CICCU was set for the *proclamation* of the gospel. They had no doubt about what that gospel was, because they trusted the authority of the Bible. So they were equally set for the *defence* of the gospel. The fact that the authority of the Bible was also crucial came home to them most of all when the gospel was at stake. Grubb quoted 1 Corinthians 15:3–4, 'For I delivered unto you first of all (*as of first importance*, NIV) that which I also received, how that Christ died for our sins according to the Scriptures; and that he was buried, and that he rose again the third day according to the Scriptures.' Through this gospel they themselves had found peace with God and new life in Christ. It was the message that God's Word, and therefore God himself, told them to preach 'as of first importance'. Any theology that took the edge off it was not just an alternative view, but a fatal weakening of the message of salvation. No-one with such beliefs could accept compromise for the sake of outward unity, friendships or theological respectability. The eternal salvation of fellow students was at stake.

No-one who saw it like that dared to alter the message, for fear that he become an enemy of men and of God. They did not deny that the liberal preachers sometimes saw conversions. So much traditional Christianity was in the background of the average ex-public schoolboy at Cambridge that the liberals were drawing on past capital. But many were not being truly converted because they had not heard a message of the 'blood of Christ' with the divine authority and the personal application of the message. Once more the CICCU men had to say, 'Here we stand; we can do no other.' They saw themselves as compelled to stand out in the starkest way for what they believed was the only message that is 'the power of God for salvation'.

Chapter 6
1920–30
Clarifying a policy

The problems were not over after the CICCU had taken its stand. And without the 1919 summer house party at Keswick there would perhaps have been shipwreck. There was no CICCU camp that year, as there was in subsequent years. However, Mrs C. T. Studd was back from Africa to be with her children and had a house party at Keswick, to which she invited a good number of CICCU men with a few from other universities. Spiritually it was rather hard going at the start. As nothing much was being accomplished, a small group met one evening for a prayer meeting for the house party. They had thought it might last about half an hour; in fact they finished at about 2am.

Norman Grubb was one of the leaders. After an exhausting battle in prayer the meeting ended with a sense of triumph and an assurance of prayer answered. They rose from their knees with joy. The whole atmosphere of the house party changed. It was a turning point for the CICCU also. As Grubb describes it, 'Faithfulness came in Cambridge, fire came at Keswick.' It was not that they had a definable, new 'second blessing' experience, but they had a new reliance on God's Holy Spirit and the plain gospel and they had been given a vision and an assurance of God's blessing. They were able to go ahead from that time with a new confidence. They were delivered from what might have become a rather negative, defensive outlook.

Many of them went on from Keswick to a very remarkable CSSM beach mission at Eastbourne, where God did an unusual work. 'For the first time I led a boy to Christ,' wrote Noel Palmer. There was a *touch* of revival as a great many young people professed conversion. The team returned to university in the autumn with a new confidence in the living power of God and his gospel.

The IVF and its Basis

Noel Palmer (always called 'Tiny' because of his enormous stature) had been recovering from wounds in a military hospital on the Backs in Cambridge since January 1919. He had been drawn into the CICCU circle and had great admiration for the friends he made there. He writes, 'I had never before seen such a group . . . They were all *men* and I hated "cissies" and prigs. These men knew and understood men, were natural and wholesome in every way. The church often put me off or left me cold; they attracted me and set me on fire.'

Nevertheless, when he went up to Oxford at Easter 1919 he drifted spiritually. He was followed by the prayers of Cambridge friends. Norman Grubb got him rather unwillingly to go to Keswick and Eastbourne, and at Keswick his life was revolutionized. The autumn term 1919, he wrote, 'was like another world. DPM and weekly Bible Readings began at once, and we soon had about forty men meeting. My rooms were so often occupied day and night by little spontaneous prayer groups that one of the men who had been accustomed to dropping in gave up in despair, and reported that "you couldn't get into Tiny's rooms nowadays without finding 'a forest of bottoms' all round the place !" (We used to kneel to pray.) Word went round that something had happened to Tiny Palmer at Wadham and that he'd gone off his head. We were lampooned in a local theatre (especially after starting open-airs at the Martyrs' Memorial). The Varsity rugger fifteen were going to throw us in the river, but the local communists drew their fire instead because they were running a huge strike meeting next to the Martyrs' Memorial.'

The result was the restarting of the OICCU with a vengeance. (It was actually called the Oxford University Bible Union for a while.) Strong links of friendship and mutual encouragement were built between the two Christian Unions in Oxford and Cambridge. Regular prayer bulletins were exchanged. This helped to give a wider vision and it was proposed to try to establish a nationwide fellowship of CUs – a plan that had been eagerly discussed at the Keswick house party. Norman Grubb was again one of the pioneers and in December 1919 a first 'Inter-Varsity Conference' was called in London. The name, incidentally, owed at least something to the fact that it was planned to start in the evening of the 'Inter-Varsity rugger match' at Twickenham. It was judged that more evangelical students would be in London that day than any other!

The conference called together students from Cambridge, several from Oxford and London and one from Durham. Only about sixty were present (all men), but it was the start of what became the 'Inter-Varsity Fellowship' (now the 'Universities and Colleges Christian Fellowship'). There and then plans were laid to start Christian Unions wherever like-minded students could be found. A letter had appeared in the religious press saying that no intelligent person any longer believed in the atonement as taught by the apostles in substitutionary terms. The six members of the CICCU Exec who were at the conference wrote a reply which was also published. They did not care whether they were considered intelligent or not; they did want to affirm that they believed this truth with all their hearts and minds.

The correspondence brought them into touch with students in one or two other centres. They appointed a committee to plan another conference – perhaps it could be an annual event. A few years later another CICCU man, H. R. Gough, was appointed travelling secretary to visit the groups and encourage them. In 1928 the Inter-Varsity Fellowship of Evangelical Unions was officially created to give substance to what was already in existence as small, often very small, CUs, started in thirteen of the universities. Between 1919 and 1933 ten out of the fifteen IVF chairmen were CICCU men and during all this time the IVF was a major 'missionary' interest of the CICCU.

All Christian Unions were to be autonomous in the new IVF and to have no obligation to find money or other support for the national fellowship. The example of SCM made them cautious. But the bond of union was to be a Doctrinal Basis which was drawn up by a small subcommittee with the help of senior friends. All Christian Unions who wished to be affiliated to the IVF had to have a Doctrinal Basis 'substantially in agreement' with it and the CICCU put a clause in their constitution to the effect that they accepted the Doctrinal Basis of the IVF. CICCU men played an important part in this development and the idea and content of the Basis owed much to some of them. The CICCU realized that a clear and explicit doctrinal statement was needed in a world in which almost all the great doctrines were being doubted or denied by leading theologians and church dignitaries.

The CICCU had nailed its doctrinal colours to the mast. It stood clearly for 'the divine inspiration and infallibility of Holy Scripture, as originally given'. It also stood without qualification for 'redemption from the guilt, penalty and power of sin only through the sacrificial death (as our Representative and Substitute) of Jesus Christ, the Incarnate Son of God'. The doctrinal position seemed quite untenable to most educated Christians. The 'baiting' of CICCU men with problems about evolution, Jonah and the flood became an entertaining pastime for many Cambridge friends. The CICCU's evangelistic zeal and devotion, however, were admired and coveted by some other groups who felt that they, perhaps, lacked in this respect. Could not the CICCU become an evangelistic arm of the SCM? The next twenty years saw constant argument about policy and the hammering out of a view of witness which in the end made official cooperation with non-evangelical bodies clearly inconsistent.

Cooperation policy

In late 1919 the CICCU were considering another Mission when the Student Christian Movement in Cambridge announced that they were planning one for the following year. They invited the CICCU to take part. At first the CICCU refused; then they decided to come in so long as their missioner did not join in any united statement of belief. The president stressed their fear lest the university 'be edified with a code of morals to observe rather than enriched by a new life', and defined once again the Christian Union's conviction 'that the Bible as originally given is, and not merely contains, the inspired Word of God, and is the only infallible guide to faith and practice; and that all are dead in sin and unable to please God until they have turned and received atonement for sin through the death of Jesus Christ and new life through His Spirit'.

It was agreed that there would be four main missioners: a Nonconformist Dr Gray; Bishop Charles Gore, who would speak in the university church of Great St Mary's; the Bishop of Peterborough (a former CICCU president, Theodore Woods), who was invited by the liberal evangelicals and who would preach in Holy Trinity where his brother Edward was vicar; and a missioner in the Guildhall where the CICCU could have their own speaker.

Time was short. The CICCU tried to get Norman Grubb's uncle, George Grubb (through whose CICCU Mission Theodore Woods had been converted as a fresher), but it was too late for him to get free, and suitable missioners were few. They eventually secured Barclay F. Buxton, the president's father, who was just home from the mission field. Theodore Woods in his open letter to the university stated his aim as follows: 'I am coming among you as a Cambridge man to talk quite plainly about the things that matter most. What the world needs in these days, what each of us needs, is to understand God and His character; to realize that in His Kingdom lies the sole hope of the world, and to discover how best we can each bring our contribution to the supreme adventure of setting it up among men.'[52] Since this gave no clear indication of preaching Christ and him crucified, and since it put the emphasis on what we could contribute rather than on the grace of God, the CICCU were not enthusiastic. They backed Buxton without qualification.

With excellent attendance (average daily total about 2,000) and many personal talks, the Mission was generally considered in Cambridge to have been a great success, *except* for the CICCU part of it. Buxton was inevitably somewhat out of touch, as he had been abroad. He was not primarily an evangelist, though he was a faithful preacher of the gospel. Also, when men had begun to be convicted in the Guildhall, they frequently went off to other missioners only to get the impression that sin and forgiveness were not the major problems. The CICCU discovered the great disadvantages of a joint mission. Nevertheless the CICCU members brought their friends to a reasonably full Guild-hall and a number did profess conversion, of whom some went on to lifelong service on the mission field. The vicar of Holy Trinity wrote, 'All groups an unbounded success except the CICCU.' The CICCU knew that numbers were not so important, so long as people were born again, and they rejoiced in the genuine results they saw.

The difference between the message of the CICCU and the others began to appear as a matter of whether the grace of God was central. Those who would not preach the death of Christ for our sins and in our place could not clearly preach a totally free grace of God, because they had no basis for totally free forgiveness. Without realizing it, a human contribution to salvation began to creep in. Men were asked to decide for Christ, or to follow Christ, rather than to trust in Christ as their Saviour and Lord – one who brought a totally undeserved salvation.

In this situation the CICCU found themselves standing as clearly over against the normal High Church teaching of the time as against the liberal teaching. That had always been the case. The liberals called the biblical doctrine of the atonement 'the theology of the slaughterhouse'. What they preached instead (largely the example and moral teaching of Christ) was undeniably popular and acceptable to their generation, but it was fatally weak as a gospel. The High Church preaching was never so popular and it made greater demands on people, but it seemed to the CICCU often to sacrifice the truth of the finished work of Christ for an offer of salvation on conditions – conditions of attendance on the ceremonies and ordinances of the church and an upright life. Works entered into it in the wrong place and again the result was that the gospel was not the gospel of free and full salvation through the death of Christ. It was not a salvation whose reality was to be proved by good works as a response of love for Christ's complete and sufficient work done for us. Certainly many 'churchy' students were trusting in their religiosity for salvation and needed to be shown that this was not the New Testament gospel and that it offered no personal relationship to God. The High Church preachers on the whole failed to make this clear, even though they might have agreed if pressed.

As a result of this Mission the CICCU lost face and lost some popular support. There was, however, one important gain. Up to this point the evangelical members of the women's colleges in Cambridge had had no organized programme of their own. They were not officially members of the university. They were not welcome at the DPM or other CICCU activities – except the Sunday night sermon, where they sat on their own in the gallery. During this Mission three or four women were converted through the help of Miss Dorothea Reader-Harris, who came up to sing and to work in the women's colleges for the CICCU (she later became Mrs Godfrey Buxton). These included the president and secretary of the Atheists' Club, who had no use for the 'soft sell' of the other religious groups. Other women were greatly helped in the Mission and there was a substantial growth of evangelical witness in the women's colleges. The Cambridge Women's Inter-Collegiate Christian Union was therefore formed and continued its strong witness until it merged with the CICCU in 1948.

The CICCU were disappointed that they had not seen greater things, but were not down-hearted. It must have taken special courage to soldier on in the face of the apparent success of the liberals and such relatively little success for the faithful preaching of biblical truth. But they believed God and persevered. Regular Sunday sermons did reach non-Christians. Friends of CICCU men were being converted and a steady flow of stalwart men went on into the ministry and the professions and out to the mission field. The CICCU was ridiculed by the religious and irreligious alike and responded by regarding other religious groups, especially the Faculty of Divinity, as imparting spiritual poison.

The CICCU seemed small and insignificant, whereas the SCM became extremely popular with undergraduates and seniors alike. While the CICCU preachers were not well known, the SCM had famous preachers every Sunday who drew very large audiences. By comparison the Sunday services of the CICCU seemed ineffective. Harold Earnshaw Smith ('Annie Smith'), who was on the Pastorate team, led the CICCU in open-air services in the market place every Sunday night in the summer term. He was a tremendous encouragement and stimulus to positive evangelism, though it must be admitted that the CICCU were often tactless and aggressive.

Meanwhile missionary interest in the CICCU was strong. In 1922 the Cambridge University Missionary Band was formed for those 'willing' to go abroad. Fifty-two joined, of whom 35 actually went abroad, and this was out of a CICCU membership of about 100. Similar groups were formed in the following years. 'Cambridge Prayer Fellowship' groups were also created for those graduating each year. These kept members in touch by circular letters two or three times a year and were a significant spiritual help to quite a few. They served to maintain a missionary and evangelistic vision and some CPFs were active continuously for more than sixty years. When the CICCU became much larger after the Second World War, the CPFs were less significant and usually functioned for only five or ten years.

In 1926 the widespread hardships in the country came to a head in the General Strike. Cambridge continued as if nothing was happening, until the week itself. Then the undergraduates were nearly all enthusiastically recruited as strike-breakers. The missionary secretary (L. F. E. Wilkinson) spent two days shifting milk-churns at Waterloo Station ('You rolled them on their edges in a rather delicate balance and we were swimming in milk by the end of the day'). He then drove a tram with a zest and fervour that even Jehu might have admired. But when it was all over they returned to the isolated world of the university with relief. It had been tremendous fun! Most students had little interest in the social questions, but there were important questions that they did understand and had to sort out in Cambridge.

The Willy Nicholson Mission

In 1926 another joint Mission was planned. This time the CICCU (now about 200 strong) chose Stuart Holden, a London vicar of great reputation and personal charm. A small group in the CICCU were fearful that he would be too eager to be nice to the other missioners and might not therefore speak clearly enough. When he signed with the other missioners a very bland letter to the university, their fears were increased. Dr Basil Atkinson (by this time an under-librarian at the university library) set himself to pray that Holden would not come. A week before the Mission Holden had to withdraw on grounds of health! There was consternation in the CICCU, because missioners were very few and they could not think of anyone suitable who was in the least likely to be free. At the CICCU camp at Keswick that summer Earnshaw Smith had introduced them to W. P. Nicholson ('Willy Nick', as the CICCU called him) and in the end they wondered if he could be God's man for the occasion. Nicholson was a rough and ready Irish evangelist, who had been a sailor before the mast and who had had a tremendous ministry among working-class people. His preaching in Northern

Ireland had had far-reaching results and led, among other things, to the starting of a CU in Queen's University, Belfast, in 1921.

The CICCU had invited Nicholson to come over for three days of Mission preparation, 'to pep us up before the Mission'. A delegation met him off the train at Euston and suggested that he should take Holden's place. Nicholson said afterwards, 'I nearly fainted. I would rather have entered a den of lions.' 'I can't talk to educated University men,' was his reply; 'I'm just a simple sailor fellow . . . but let's have a word of prayer.' So they prayed there and then on the Euston station platform and Nicholson threw his hat in the air and shouted, 'Praise the Lord!' Nicholson telegraphed to Ireland and found that the week concerned was one of the few in the whole year in which he could be free. So his name was put by the CICCU to the united Mission committee for approval. No-one present had ever heard of him, and the one member who had and who would probably have objected could not be present that day. So Nicholson became the CICCU missioner alongside Bishop William Temple and a prominent liberal Free Churchman, Cyril Norwood.

Willy Nicholson was a totally different man from Stuart Holden. He was extremely hard hitting, blunt about sin and hell, and with a racy and uncultured sense of humour. Despite his social unease in the presence of 'University men', he had absolutely no fear of human opinions and knew virtually nothing about universities. He did know about sin and salvation and preached with the authority of the Word of God. At the united introductory meeting, with the president of the Union Society[53] in the chair, he upset even some of the CICCU by his bluntness. Nicholson stated that he had been born again on a particular date and then, baldly and with little comment, affirmed the whole of the Apostles' Creed sentence by sentence. William Temple shook him warmly by the hand as they left the platform, but the Free Church minister appeared deliberately to turn his back on him as a public gesture. As they walked away across the market place Earnshaw Smith said to Nicholson, 'Whatever made you do that? Now you have ruined everything.' 'Brother Smith,' replied Nicholson, 'if I had done what you thought, and pleased everybody, it would have been the end of your Mission. Now you will see. God will work.'

On the Sunday, the first day, Nicholson preached to a rather small audience in Holy Trinity Church on the text 'Ye must be born again'. Crowds attended the other missioners. But at least Nicholson was not dull. 'It was extraordinary,' said one freshman; 'very vulgar and yet – very attractive at the same time.' He lashed out against the popular idea that Christianity was just following the example of Christ. He hammered away at the biblical truth that 'You must be born again' and a few professed conversion that night.

The reputation of the missioner in Holy Trinity began to spread. His style and manners were highly unconventional. Students came just for fun and then were either offended or convicted, though some mocked. The president of the Drunks' Club was converted – later to become secretary of a missionary society – and brought his friends along too. Each night there were some who made a profession of conversion. And Willy Nicholson didn't make it easy. The Mission ended in a cloud of controversy, but with a substantial number of new Christians.

The issues becoming clearer

The Cambridge scene was never quite the same after that. CICCU men either left in disillusionment and joined the SCM, or realized afresh the impossibility of compromise and the need to speak clearly of God's truth, however unpopular that might be. The other societies were also different in their attitude to the CICCU. Many were angry that such a witness had been given in such a way. They were no longer enthusiastic for future cooperation; indeed, they had little desire to be associated with that kind of Christianity. To them the CICCU seemed out of place in a university. Nevertheless, attendance at the Sunday night evangelistic sermons increased. In 1928 Charles Raven, a leading liberal evangelical (who became the Regius Professor of Divinity in 1932), wrote of the CICCU, 'It is incredible that anyone with the intelligence to pass Littlego (the university entrance exam) should still believe in Jonah's whale and Balaam's ass.'[54] Such attitudes were common.

For its part the CICCU was getting used to this kind of attack. Liberalism was becoming more and more aridly negative. Theological study did not even pretend to be much of a preparation for the ministry. It was more of an academic philosophical exercise for the solving of intellectual problems. To study theology was to enter a spiritual wilderness, personally enlivened only by a few lecturers like Raven, who was warm and enthusiastic and had great power of oratory, but little biblical content to his lectures. Most of the CICCU men who took theology seriously became liberal and were lost to the cause. Those who survived, with a few notable exceptions, were people who laughed their way through the course and nurtured their spirits in the CICCU and in vacation evangelism among young people. There was little else they could do. There were virtually no evangelical theological scholars who could help and no literature except what could be dismissed as long out of date.

Nevertheless, in the growing fellowship of the IVF they began to find friends in other universities. Even if there was none in Cambridge, there were university professors (notably in science and medicine) elsewhere who would come and speak. There were older men in the parishes and in the Keswick circle, too, who were willing to do all they could to help, though their number was not large.

In its turn the CICCU contributed substantially to the IVF. The first four IVF travelling secretaries (1923–9) were all CICCU men.[55] Hugh Gough, for instance, had been president of the CICCU for nearly two years (1925–7) and travelled widely in the following year to help the new evangelical groups emerging in universities all round the country. The incipient Manchester CU, consisting of four students, wrote of his visit in 1927, 'We felt that God had sent Mr Gough to us as an encouragement from the Evangelical Unions already formed, and we thanked God and took courage.' The following week the Manchester University Evangelical Union was launched. News of the CICCU's witness also helped in other places. They corresponded with students as far away as Aberdeen and a CICCU member finishing his studies in Edinburgh contributed to the start of the EU there in 1922.[56]

At Oxford in 1928 the OICCU got going again. It had lapsed in 1925 into being the 'Devotional Union' within the SCM and that had never been a success. Now sixteen members broke away from SCM and restarted the OICCU. There was intense interest and prayer support in Cambridge following the IVF conference where they had met. For their first public outreach three CICCU men, including the president, Kenneth Hooker, were asked over to speak at a meeting in the Town Hall on 'What Christ means to me'. The Town Hall was packed and the OICCU was re-launched with a new confidence in God – the collection at the door exactly meeting the formidable expenses to the nearest penny! Having learnt its lesson by painful experience, the OICCU quickly became an enthusiastic and robustly evangelical group again and joined with the CICCU and the LIFCU (London) in helping to found CUs all over the British Isles.

If the CICCU helped to establish the IVF, the IVF helped the CICCU to remain faithful and to be more confident of the gospel. In Cambridge, where they were a despised minority, it was a help to know of friends in other universities who stood for the same witness and policy.[57]

Oxford, Cambridge and London were the three largest British universities. A CICCU man, Chris Maddox, became the IVF (honorary spare-time) missionary secretary and travelled the Unions in a minute and ancient car to stir up missionary enthusiasm. Others helped in other ways.

In 1928 Norman Grubb came back from Canada and challenged the infant IVF to do something to start similar work there. An IVF income of £20 per annum hardly seemed adequate! But the same autumn the sacrifice of fellow students (who sold belongings to finance the trip) and the help of Professor Rendle Short (Professor of Surgery at Bristol) sent Dr Howard Guinness (Bart's Hospital, London) across the Atlantic to Canada.

Professor Rendle Short belonged to the 'Open Brethren' and was an indefatigable visitor to tiny groups of students to help CUs to get going. He was a constant visitor and speaker at Cambridge and did much to inspire the vision of a nationwide network of Christian Unions and to give a sense of responsibility for helping other universities and other countries. This was needed because Cambridge could easily forget everyone else, except perhaps the OICCU.

In 1929, when Howard Guinness went on to Australia, Kenneth Hooker, who had been CICCU President in 1927–8, went to Canada for a year as their first staff worker. In 1930 he was followed by 'Tiny' Palmer of Oxford for three years until a Canadian worker was found. Thus the Canadian IVF was established and later pioneered the work in USA. The foundations of the International Fellowship of Evangelical Students were being laid and CICCU members had an honourable part in helping in several countries.

Superspirituality

During the same period the CICCU had to resist the impact of the movement led by Frank Buchman that at first was called 'The First Century Christian Fellowship'. Later it was called the Oxford Group and then Moral Rearmament (MRA). It tested the CICCU's discernment to the limit.

Buchman was an American of great personal charm. He had arrived in 1920 and made Cambridge his base for a year. He constantly stated his faith in the whole Bible, the death of Christ and the second coming. He spoke of blessing that he had received at Keswick. But although he seemed to be biblical, he rarely spoke from the Bible. He disapproved of holding a Bible or speaking from it directly, as he said it might put off worldly people. His talks were very thrilling and he had round him men and women keen to win souls by using his methods. He gave impressive reports of revival in American universities. He was impatient of formality or unreality in religion. He stressed the need for a personal moment-by-moment experience and fellowship with the Lord, and his followers were active personal evangelists.

Buchman was at first received warmly by the CICCU. His challenge to an absolute morality was needed and helpful. Many CICCU men owed something to his emphases. He took the CICCU weekend and one of their house parties. As time went on, however, disturbing features emerged. He spoke of the Quiet Time, but it was less and less a time of Bible study and prayer and increasingly a time of 'listening to God'. This members did with their mind blank and with paper and pencil in hand, writing down the thoughts that came to them. In this way men received entirely irrational guidance about the most trivial as well as the most important issues, and such guidance was regarded as authoritative. Guidance at other times was instant and unpredictable. The leader of a student team would decide only at the last minute who should speak at the Open-air. Either this was very spiritual indeed, or it was a pious cloak for indecisiveness and a refusal to be guided by the discipline of biblical wisdom.

'Sharing', especially sharing of sins, was also a prominent feature. The whole movement sounded more 'spiritual' than anything based on the Bible. Quite often guidance was received for other people, dictating to them what they should do. Confession of sins in public became a feature and the fellowship of sinners seemed to be warmer than the fellowship of saints. But the problem came to a head when secondary issues began to take the place of the gospel. The MRA's Four Absolutes (absolute honesty, absolute purity, absolute unselfishness and absolute love) became the point of challenge to the non-Christian. The result was that, when men and women were 'changed', it often proved to be purely an attempt at personal moral revolution. Spectacular converts who spoke in public proved soon to be spectacular backsliders. Only a few seemed to be truly born again and 'the Groups' produced a fierce antagonism among non-Christians, so that Christians had to be willing to take sides. The Groups left something of a scorched earth behind them and many Christians felt they had to dissociate themselves entirely from their aggressive but biblically weak approach.

Many people in the CICCU were involved at least for a time. They tended to lose their concern for doctrine and to end up less definite about the gospel – unless they reacted against 'the Groups', as a considerable proportion did. But the unqualified challenge was a help to some – so long as they did not lose their biblical base. Gradually the CICCU and 'the Groups' drifted apart and became distinct entities; the latter shifted their emphasis to Oxford, where they were rather more successful. This gave rise to the title 'Oxford Group'. The influence continued in Cambridge for a while, however. Ivor Beauchamp (son of one of the Cambridge Seven) wrote in 1922, 'Frank Buchman held one of his week-end house parties in John's; it was a time of real power and blessing and a great stimulus to those of us who went.' He then named two recent CICCU ex-presidents as having been present.[58]

In 1924 Douglas Johnson, a student at King's College and later King's College Hospital, London, became secretary of the Inter-Varsity Conference. His predecessor, an Oxford man, had become favourable to Buchman. 'DJ', as he was always called, saw the danger and helped others to do so. DJ's ministry was never in the foreground; but his lively vision, clarity of principle and determination that the men on the spot should carry the responsibility were an enormous help to many in the CICCU over a long period. A number of former CICCU leaders who were then finishing their medical studies in London were still influential in Cambridge at that time. There was a good deal of coming and going between Cambridge and London, especially from the London medical schools, and DJ was at the centre of the London CU scene and the growing IVF. Many of the leaders of the new CUs had too little discernment to see the danger. DJ was one of those who did.

Harold Earnshaw Smith, who was in Cambridge for most of this period in the Pastorate and in other capacities, was another steadying influence. He was never a traditionalist and was full of mischief. He nevertheless always kept his priorities right and helped many others to do the same.

The CICCU leadership especially owed a great deal to him.

'The Groups' returned to Cambridge in strength in 1929–32 and became influential with some support from deans and chaplains. They presented a choice between 'orthodoxy and life'. Why cling to orthodoxy if the Groups offered life? But their influence soon waned as the fruits of their work were seen on the whole to be ephemeral. Many people were helped by their challenge; but in those cases where the response lasted and grew into something lifelong, it was for the most part among people who already had a good biblical basis for their faith or who maintained a discipline of Bible study and Bible exposition.

In these ways the CICCU, in fellowship with the other CUs in the IVF, hammered out a policy. It became increasingly clear that cooperation with bodies that did not have the same witness was not only unfruitful and inconsistent, but harmful to the clarity and authority of the gospel. The CICCU were not prepared for the gospel to be seen as just one human point of view among other more rational or more 'traditional' alternatives. They had to be distinctive and clear, and free to get on with a frankly Bible-based ministry. They had to stand against liberalism on the one hand and an unbiblical superspirituality on the other.

Such a policy was not easily maintained. There was constant pressure for the CICCU, the college groups and the CUs in other universities to treat their doctrinal stance as less important, so that they could have joint activities and official fellowship. Generation after generation of students had to think it out and decide whether the truths at issue were important enough to necessitate a distinctive witness. The key concept was 'witness'; what do we stand for and what is our public witness? It affected the Membership Basis, the Doctrinal Basis for committee members and speakers, and any joint platform with other theologies. Every year there were some who disagreed and put their energies more into the SCM than the CU. But many of those who concluded that they must be distinctive have gone on to be leaders in the church and have been valiant for truth in key positions around the world.

Chapter 7
1930–45
The turn of the tide

By 1930 the CICCU was established as a minority group. Their theology was laughed at and they were not taken very seriously by most religious or intellectual people, though their zeal and sincerity were admired. They were regarded as anti-intellectual, anti-theological and obscurantist, clinging tenaciously to outmoded beliefs simply because they were afraid to face the facts. All this was in a university that was a far more self-consciously intellectual community than it is today. Those who were influential in the student world were on the whole more intellectual, particularly in religious and anti-religious circles. Skill in sport was still highly rated, but intellectual ability was, for most people, more important. There were some idle (and usually wealthy) students reading for ordinary degrees and doing as little work as possible, but their numbers were steadily declining.

Cambridge still had much of a glorified boarding school atmosphere. The majority of students did come from boarding schools and, of the rest, many were very middle class. The debating atmosphere of a good sixth form was continued at Cambridge, with the addition of the added intellectual confidence given by a few years. As one student put it, 'When I came up to Cambridge, I thought that all intellectual problems were pretty well settled and that our generation knew most of what one needed to know. It took me three years to discover how ignorant I was.'

Guests had to be out of college or lodgings by 10pm. Unless by special permission, all undergraduates had to be in by midnight. Cap and gown had to be worn outside college after dark or one was liable to be fined 6s. 8d. by a proctor. Hospitality was formal. Almost everyone dined in Hall at least five evenings a week (you had to pay for that anyway) and most people sat in approximately the same place night after night with the same group of friends and acquaintances.

In this context enthusiastic Christianity was frowned on. CICCU members were regarded as embarrassingly eccentric and their personal evangelism was in rather bad taste. They were at best a curiosity, like those frighteningly clever and hard-working students from provincial grammar schools, who were beginning to win more and more of the college scholarships. To go to chapel was reasonable, though not many went; but to be an active CICCU member was crazy. The minority of ex-grammar schoolboys were more serious minded and there were excellent Christians among them; but they rarely took the lead in the CICCU, or in other societies, because it took them a year or so to be at home in the new, alien atmosphere of this residential community. The ex-grammar schoolboys, however, began to have a healthy broadening influence on the social base and outlook of the CICCU as well as of the rest of the university. During the war the university became distinctively and irreversibly less 'public school' and less Church of England, and the CICCU followed suit.

Basil Atkinson

There were practically no senior members of the university who would associate with the CICCU. Of the seniors, Basil Atkinson alone came regularly to the DPM and threw his bachelor house open on Tuesday nights for open discussion.[59] 'Basil At' provided a major influence for a strong doctrinal policy over many years to 1970, when he became a sick man (he died in 1971). In the early 1920s he had seemed rather erratic and too dogmatic about what was God's will for the CICCU. Earnshaw Smith had been a wiser and more inspiring adviser. But in the 1930s Basil At became a much appreciated elder statesman. He did not now try to dictate to the CICCU; instead, he advised. Occasionally he urged a point; generally he prayed privately and exercised his influence by friendship. He had an explosive sense of humour and was himself the subject of endless jokes. Because the CICCU laughed at him, they did not find his influence oppressive and he was greatly respected and loved. Each term he took three or four weekly college Bible studies, so most members benefited from his Bible exposition. He was an excellent Greek scholar, decidedly against Roman Catholicism and enthusiastic for evangelical truth. His views were sometimes quaint, always sincere. When someone prayed in a prayer meeting for the pope who was ill, and added that the pope had done so much good, Basil exploded with a vehement 'No!' Many, many students owed their continued doctrinal orthodoxy to his help and prayers.

Another supportive figure was Archdeacon Guillebaud, home in Cambridge from Ruanda for part of the period. His house on Barton Road was a centre of lively discussion and (marvellously and helpfully) a place where the CICCU men and women could meet naturally at least for the huge Sunday buffet lunches that Mrs G. provided.

He was a scholarly Bible translator. Basil At provided some stimulus to deeper Bible study.

Christy Innes, an Aberdeen graduate studying at Westminster College (the Presbyterian theological college in Cambridge), and John Wenham helped to get the Theological Students Prayer Union going in Cambridge. The TSPU (later the Theological Students Fellowship) meetings drew theologs and a number of non-theologs. It later became the RTSF (the Religious and Theological Studies Fellowship). It helped greatly towards a more positive desire to get the best out of theological study and steadied many waverers.

Dr R. E. D. Clark, a chemistry research student and demonstrator, started with others an apologetics discussion group. This was never quite accepted by the CICCU hierarchy, but it helped some to a less anti-intellectual stance. This started in 1929 with papers by Basil Atkinson and F. D. Coggan (later Archbishop of Canterbury) among others, and continued in a spasmodic way up until 1940.

Campers

Meanwhile the evangelism went on. Camps for public schoolboys, especially the 'Bash Camps' (led by 'Bash', the Revd E. J. H. Nash), sent up to Cambridge a remarkable stream of freshers who already had some skill in evangelism. They emphasized the 'simple gospel' and, being trained in work with schoolboys, were sometimes rather anti-intellectual and anti-theological. That gradually righted itself for most of them, however, as they gained experience. Their ablest men became intellectually and theologically some of the more adventurous and effective evangelists and teachers of the next generation. They were also excellent personal evangelists. At one time it was a joke that to be a member of the university hockey team it was necessary either to be a CICCU member or to attend

CICCU sermons. The reason was that a 'Bash camper' was the captain of hockey and brought all the members of the team along to the Sunday night sermons – often trailing in a little late because he (and the secretary, also a Christian) had been rounding up a straggler.

In the years 1935–9 the four CICCU presidents were all 'Bash campers' and this created some restlessness, though they were good presidents. Like every other fellowship-within-a-fellowship, the 'campers' could be a bit over-whelming and they irritated some people of other outlooks and backgrounds by their special emphasis and their con-centration on men from the 'best' schools. But the CICCU owed much to them and they were reliable in policy and doctrine. They also brought a fresh concern for the min-istry at home as opposed to abroad. Some regarded this as a dangerous diversion from missionary interest, but in fact it supplemented the concern for overseas service rather than competing with it. Many of these men went on to Ridley Hall and helped CICCU college groups in a pas-toral capacity, sometimes leading their group Bible studies. Some had a deep influence for good year by year on the young Christians and new converts. This was especially true where they helped humbly and prayerfully and gave them friendship. They also helped the CICCU to be more tactful.

Background factors

At this time, however, the evangelical world was suffering from an intellectual inferiority complex. A fresher in 1938 was warned in a friendly way by an older and slightly re-bellious CICCU man not to advertise his interest in con-temporary poetry, lest he be regarded as unsound. This was not fair, but it had some truth in it.[60] Many were fright-ened of intellectual activity.

The evangelical world generally seemed to be in decline.

Many of its ablest young men and women were going liberal or losing their faith at university. At Cambridge it seemed that more were being lost to the cause than were being gained through conversion. In the year 1939–40 a CICCU member calculated that only about a dozen had professed conversion through the CICCU, though in fact there were probably considerably more.

The number of strong evangelical churches in the country was small. Many traditionally evangelical churches had now become liberal. The range of suitable speakers was therefore limited. Brethren influence was still quite strong and a number of the most articulate CICCU members came from that background. They seemed to keep to an orthodox faith in this difficult period better than many of the Anglican majority. Few of the Brethren students, of course, studied theology in the aggressively liberal theological faculty, and they were also helped by the fact that their tradition was in any case staunchly independent of prevailing religious opinions. Very few students came up from the independent churches that nowadays supply some fine leadership. CICCU was mainly Church of England or Brethren with a mere handful of others.

The university as a whole was cynical about religion. Life was easygoing. The undergraduates believed that they comprised an elite and were correspondingly rather conceited and self-satisfied. Hitler's doings on the Continent were shocking but far away. The student body in general was apathetic about religion and did not wish to discuss its verities. Probably the situation has rarely been quite so difficult. Yet men and women were won for Christ in a steady flow and a growing number entered the ministry.

In June 1939 Cambridge was the venue for a great international conference. It was convened by the IVF and its overseas associated movements which later formed the International Fellowship of Evangelical Students. The

Scandinavians chartered a ship and brought 600 over. The CICCU provided numerous guides and some of the organizers. Many of its members were made aware of the international scene in a new way and in the following years played an active part in the IFES. But the clouds of war were gathering quickly. Some of those who came from the Continent warned others that war was inevitable. They realized that very shortly numerous conference members were likely to be killed. It was, of course, only two months before the war began.

Munich and the Second World War

The Munich crisis had come just before term began in 1938 and even in the university the increasing likelihood of war had begun to be realized during the year following. Student life, however, did not change until the war began in 1939. Then courses were immediately shortened and call-up began in earnest. Conscientious objectors, including some of the CICCU men, began to face tribunals. They were supported by Basil Atkinson, who had been imprisoned in the First World War as a conscientious objector.

Throughout the Second World War the university continued in considerable strength. Military units were quartered in parts of some colleges and six-month courses began for Forces' cadets. These latter were fully part of the university and effective witness was made among them. Freshers' squashes had to be held twice a year, some at Easter and others in October as usual. Evangelistic work began to be more fruitful. Perhaps life was more serious than in the cynical 1930s. The CICCU became smaller but more compact, with about 150 members – it had 230 official members in 1937 and 130 in 1943–4. With that membership the committee knew everyone, at least by sight. And God worked. A remarkable freshers' sermon in

1941 saw about twenty professions of conversion. This was a new phenomenon for the CICCU and a number of those converted became well known in the Christian world. A rather raw Forces' cadet straight from school came up for an Air Force course. He joined the Air Force because he could think of nothing better than to be killed soon. And if he were going to die soon, he might as well do it with zest. He was converted through Derek Podmore, another Forces' cadet, an ordinand in the CICCU. When Podmore was killed in action, the new convert, who survived, went on to a fruitful ministry in the Church of England. There were many like him.

Several London colleges were evacuated to Cambridge for the duration of the war. The London School of Economics Christian Union, which had died out, was re-started with CICCU help and met in a member's college room for some time. Bedford College, Bart's Hospital Medical School and part of University College London all had flourishing CUs before long, making good use of the CICCU sermons and Bible Readings and seeing several professions of conversion.

It was not a promising time for new developments and yet certain important new trends set in. A very capable group of men were up studying theology, led by the older than usual president of 1942.[61] A high percentage of first-class degrees in theology went to CICCU men in the next few years. This gave a new confidence and the old, rather defensive attitudes began to give way to a more confident and even aggressive theological outlook. Men were being won over from a liberal to a conservative theology. Some of the most hostile teachers of theology began to change their tone.

Tyndale House was bought by the IVF in 1942 to be a centre of biblical research in Cambridge. It became a place where there were nearly always some capable postgraduates of theological acumen available for consultation. Tyndale House bore witness to two things. First, it was the fruit of the conviction that theology was now so liberal that men of conservative convictions had little chance of getting accepted for research in most universities. Research students were also being pushed into work on the most 'dry' topics – far removed from biblical studies or doctrinal studies. Evangelical research was needed to recapture the field, but it would often have to be outside the university system. Secondly, Tyndale House was sited in Cambridge because there the old tradition of more objective biblical scholarship was still as strong as anywhere in the United Kingdom. The faculty was liberal, but willing to give a first-class degree to any man who was good. They were also willing to help men to do serious scholarly textual study, though they might not help them to get research grants if they were conservative.

During the war another group of research students in the CICCU and some older undergraduates began to meet to discuss apologetic questions, especially questions on science and faith. They discovered that they could do at least as well at this kind of activity as the more liberal groups and, encouraged by the IVF, a first conference for the Research Scientists' Christian Fellowship was called by some CICCU men (including R. E. D. Clark) and met in Cambridge.

Growth and development

In other ways also the tide began to turn. The CICCU became rather more adventurous, in spite of the youth of its members, when few were up for more than two years. Some apologetics lectures, begun as an experiment, did not come off, however, because of the lack of experience. But at least they tried.

The SCM was now weak among undergraduates and

the CICCU was becoming a little more mature and less shrill. The chapels and the SCM, with their overwhelming senior support, still provided a strong alternative. The Methodist Society became the largest religious body in Cambridge and ran a series of group meetings that some CICCU members found more attractive than the CICCU college Bible studies. The latter were still largely monologues by Basil Atkinson or one of the Ridley men. But towards the end of this period experiments were being carried out in the colleges with an interactive discussion style of Bible study. Before long this became a general pattern, with perhaps one term in three devoted to a series of Bible readings given by Basil Atkinson or another more senior Christian. The change was helpful and led to a more active searching of the Scriptures by the ordinary member for himself.

IVF books had begun to appear. Archdeacon Guillebaud and G. T. Manley (now in a parish) produced the first edition of *Search the Scriptures* (1934–7) with the CICCU partly in mind. Although it was not devotional enough for some and never caught on universally in the CICCU, it helped many to go deeper than the rather superficial devotional guides they had been using. *In Understanding be Men* (a handbook on Christian doctrine) and other Inter-Varsity Press books began to supply the need for doctrine and apologetics and provided some important help in the field of evangelical literature at a student level.

John Stott was a student from 1940 to 1945 and already showed unusual gifts. The CICCU Exec, however, had the sense to send one of their number to tell him that they would not invite him to join the next committee as they believed he should be free from committee meetings. They wanted him to get on with the evangelistic and pastoral work in which he was exercising an outstanding ministry. As the Exec met for a whole evening and a substantial time of prayer on Sunday morning each week, as well as involving members in a range of other obligations, this was a sensible policy. It illustrates the fact that the real work of the CICCU was often not carried out by officers or committees. The whole effectiveness of the CICCU depended on the fact that a high proportion of ordinary members, both then and in almost all periods of its history, were active in personal evangelism and in helping one another in every way. The committee were very much looked up to and their example was influential; but they were not the CICCU, and the tone of each college group was the major influence.

At this time the Sunday morning Bible Reading was changed to Saturday night, and this gave the speaker much greater scope. In any case, Sunday mornings always tempted people to skip church and to come straight to the Bible Reading at 12.30pm from an early morning college chapel Communion and a time of personal quiet. Now more people went to local churches on Sunday mornings and the Saturday night speakers had a longer time in which to speak.

The great evangelistic opportunity was the Sunday night sermon. When the blackout was enforced and Holy Trinity was for a while no longer available, there was anxiety as to what to do. The only suitable blacked-out hall was the Dorothy Café ballroom, and that was very expensive. As the Exec were discussing it, the secretary returned to his room to find on his desk an anonymous cash gift from a student for the right amount for one week's rent. They booked the ballroom and continued there until Holy Trinity was available again, money coming in as needed. Many continued to be converted in a steady, though not spectacular, stream. The CICCU members learnt biblical truth and life in a warm fellowship of active witness; this contrasted sharply with the formality and coldness of most of the chapels and the more intellectual, but usually spiritually sterile, debates at the SCM. The 'Meth. Soc.' and the Baptist Society ('The Robert Hall Society') stood between the two, providing a mixed diet of biblical and liberal speakers and activities. Holy Trinity Church had very few strongly biblical preachers and the CICCU stalwarts went increasingly to St Paul's Church. It was not until late in the war that the 'Round Church' also began to attract evangelical students, as it gradually took over from the rather more distant St Paul's as the main CICCU church in the late 1950s. By the 1970s there was a far wider choice of biblical ministry and CICCU members were widely distributed in the churches in Cambridge.

Whether people were clever or athletic did not matter so much any more. Life was too short. It mattered only that people were genuine and the CICCU provided a transparently sincere fellowship in evangelism and Bible study. Friendships were strong and lasting. New converts were drawn into a lively and warm community for a while and then scattered to the battlefields and wartime research establishments of the world. A prayer fellowship for ex-members in the Forces was strong and, with the CICCU ex-members list, this helped to form part of the nucleus of the Graduates' Fellowship of the IVF which was created in 1941. In 1941 and 1942 the IVF annual conference was held at Cambridge and more CICCU members than usual attended, with considerable benefit to the CICCU. These gatherings had the effect also of making senior members of the university treat the CICCU more seriously.

In a difficult time the CICCU members seemed to have an uncommon spiritual vitality. They had a faith adequate to the prospect of death and it was a faith to live by. A number of people were helped by the question that, in any case, posed itself in the occasional air raid: 'Am I ready to die, and what is my confidence if I am called to stand before God tonight?' One fresher came back after a CICCU Sunday sermon and a personal talk, saying to his friend the next day, 'Yes, I am trusting Christ for my forgiveness. I am ready to die in an air raid tonight.' Of those who bothered to attend college chapel, a growing percentage turned out to be CICCU members. But the chapel fraternity was a distinct group as a rule, with not too much overlap. CICCU people attended chapel because it was the official religion, as a public witness and in order to get to know other people who might be looking for a vital faith and whom CICCU might be able to help. They did not often regularly attend the other activities of the chapel group. The majority of members abstained from alcohol and rarely went to the cinema or the theatre. At the time, of course, this reflected the traditions of the evangelical churches and the youth movements, such as Crusaders, which each year sent up a strong contingent of Christian freshers. The chaplains' traditional hospitality was a sherry party and the CICCU tended to avoid this and even the chapel breakfast after Communion, because it could interfere with the Quiet Time.

The Doctrinal Basis

Cambridge, however, remained curiously remote from the war and was bombed only slightly on two or three occasions. Everyone was busy with trying to keep things going on the reduced scale that alone was possible. The CICCU members were inevitably younger and some college groups were led by very recent converts. It was decided, therefore, that the college reps must be asked to agree a short doctrinal statement if they were not to be at the mercy of liberal or High Church influence. Yet some of the people in view were so young in the faith that their signature of the whole

Doctrinal Basis could not be a carefully thought-out agreement. In the end it was agreed to ask the college reps to sign that 'in accepting the responsibilities of membership of the General Committee, I agree to recognize the doctrinal basis of the IVFEU [the IVF of Evangelical Unions, its full title] as being the standard of doctrine and as determining the policy of the General Committee of the CICCU: and I will undertake to support only such matters as are fully consistent with it.' This worked well and prevented the college groups from inviting unsuitable speakers and from being over-influenced by powerful personalities of another view.

The policy issues were clear. As a war-time Exec memorandum stated, 'our attitude therefore to doctrines contrary to Scripture cannot be one of approval or toleration. We have got to say boldly that they are false as judged, not by our own opinion, but by the objective standards of Scripture. There is therefore a fundamental divergence of belief with a number of Christian bodies. Some deny the final authority of Scripture implicitly by saying that every "point of view" is good . . . to co-operate with such bodies is ourselves implicitly to deny the final authority of Scripture . . .'

This had to be argued out constantly because of the unremitting pressure for cooperation from chaplains and above all from the SCM. It seemed a tiresome and time-wasting occupation to go over the issues again and again; yet those who were forced to think them out became some of the most reliable and consistent evangelical Christians in their future life and work.

Defence and proclamation

The CICCU had learnt to call heresy by its name and on the whole they did so graciously. They believed themselves to be set for the defence and proclamation of the gospel.

They ran a Mission every three years, though these were not, at this stage, very fruitful efforts. There seemed to be no wholly suitable missioners available and the painstaking personal evangelism of the members and the Sunday sermons were more fruitful than the Missions. Each Mission, however, did reach a number who probably would not otherwise have heard the gospel. On the other hand, a very big Mission and the other activities run by the SCM seemed to achieve little, for the message was neither clear nor biblical. Gradually the CICCU began to be a major religious force in the undergraduate world once again. Though few people could see it at the time, the tide had turned. This was not because the CICCU was better or stronger, but because the alternatives to a biblical Christianity were being tried and found wanting in the fires of war and its aftermath.

People, once again, were willing to listen to an old-fashioned biblical message. The theological faculty of the time would have laughed at the suggestion. They were quite sure that only a liberal/rationalistic approach could help the 'modern man'. The official representatives of religion mostly wrote the CICCU off as schoolboy religion which would fade out in due time. But not many were so hotly antagonistic as before. The more ecumenical spirit was against opposing anything. On the other hand, the seniors were not as likely to have a basic sympathy with evangelical religion as in the 1920s. At the undergraduate level, however, the CICCU was rapidly gaining ground and getting a much better hearing. Whatever the seniors said, the undergraduate with a spiritual need or with an awakened conscience tended to turn much more often to the CICCU to try to understand what it was saying.

The life of a CICCU member

The active CICCU member's Christian life had, at this period, three main focal points. First, the Quiet Time was widely observed. Probably almost everyone set aside at least 20 minutes, some an hour or more, for personal prayer and Bible study every day. There was considerable emphasis on this, both officially and unofficially.

Secondly, the college group was, in contrast with earlier times, the focus of fellowship. In 1937 these groups ranged from twenty-five to two in membership. But some non-members and a few non-Christians came regularly to the Bible studies. In every college there was a weekly Bible study and also a weekly prayer meeting attended by the majority of the members. Some of the college groups had breakfast together once a week before the prayer meeting.

The college representative's task was overwhelmingly pastoral and a good rep would get round his members, have prayer with them and encourage them in evangelism and in the Christian life. The lines were drawn tightly on the question of amusement (drink, dancing, theatre and cinema). But as one non-Christian observer remarked, 'The CICCU seems to be the best social club in the university.' What he meant was that it drew in people of all faculties and types (although there were no women members) in a fellowship that was transparently genuine. The friendships were formed mostly on a college basis (sometimes on a faculty basis, especially in medicine and science). There was much mutual challenge to go all out and win others for Christ. Among the more active, anyone who did not have a friend to bring to a Sunday service felt something of a failure. These friends were prayed for by name in college prayer meetings. The pressure to bring someone to sermons was probably sometimes overdone. A more natural witness could probably have been as effective and less stressful, but they were deeply in earnest and the quieter and less activist members found a natural and positive role within the fellowship.

Thirdly, beyond the college circle, many members went to central activities. A fairly high proportion went to the DPM once or twice a week. Third-year members often took freshers under their wing and introduced them to the various central activities, such as the DPM and the weekend Bible reading and the Saturday night prayer meeting which focused on the Sunday sermon. That included many personal prayers for non-Christians and was a stirring experience, with Basil Atkinson's urgent and sometimes quaint prayers which encouraged others to pray aloud, even if they could not express themselves in elegant language.

The weekend Bible Reading was a school of Christian teaching such as was rarely available in churches or anywhere else. Many members learnt far more than they realized at the time from this weekly exercise. The Sunday night evangelistic sermons also helped to form a clear idea of the gospel. The great opportunity of personal talks afterwards was a practical school of evangelism and the means of conversion for many.

Study was taken seriously by the Christians on the whole and a certain amount of Christian reading was fairly widely encouraged and practised. There were still some who did as little work as possible so as to be free for evangelism (and sport). Some regarded this as the best training for missionary or pastoral ministry. But as life became more serious, concern to do well at work also became more general. Speakers such as Professor Rendle Short from less ivory-tower universities helped in this and deliberately made this point from time to time. But as has always been the case in a residential university, an enormous amount of time was spent, much of it profitably, in personal discussion and debate with both Christians and non-Christians. The CICCU was not cliquish. Nearly all the members had quite a few non-Christian friends. But the closest friendships were nearly all within the circle of other CICCU members.

Social concern

In the early 1920s the lines between the CICCU and the SCM had been definite, but not so tightly drawn as to prevent some of the leaders from holding office in both societies (e.g. Stephen Neill and Max Warren, who were both to become international missionary statesmen). As the SCM became more clearly the voice of liberal theology, this became impossible. In this there were some important gains. The witness of the CICCU and its leaders became clearer doctrinally. That was essential to evangelism, because the biblical gospel needed to be sharply contrasted with the liberal gospel. But at the same time the CICCU men could become too isolated and their faith a little brittle as a result. They might never meet and debate with others while at Cambridge, but they were sure to have to do so when they went down, and some were not well prepared for that. There was also on both sides a danger of overreaction against a caricature of the other. After a while the CICCU leaders began to take the initiative in making personal contact with SCM leaders, and that helped.

The question of social involvement was probably the outstanding example. The SCM spent a lot of its energy in discussing social questions. This had been one of the differences between them and the CICCU way back in 1910, although it had not been the major question of debate. Now it loomed bigger. Was social concern in the SCM a cause or a symptom of its weakness on the gospel? It had started in the SCM as a desire to apply the Bible to social questions; by 1935 what the SCM was doing was open to criticism as being neither well based on the Bible nor dealing with actual questions for the student. It also distracted from evangelism. The SCM was led by older men who tried to run its programme as if it were a ministers' fraternal. Even the strong influence of William Temple in the central councils of the SCM meant that it was often talking about questions that were quite outside the experience of students.

In 1933 Basil Atkinson re-edited *Old Paths in Perilous Times* (see p. 86) and copies were given free to all CICCU freshers. A comparatively mild statement in the first edition was reprinted in the second edition: 'no amount of reform will raise a man one degree from spiritual blindness and degradation; it may even make harder the humiliation involved in accepting Christianity. The plan which God has ordained is regeneration.' But in the second edition a new paragraph was added: 'While believing that it is always a part of Christian duty to ameliorate distress, the CICCU cannot be enthusiastic about schemes for bringing world peace by means of political bodies such as the League of Nations, or social uplift by methods of reform. It holds that in the Gospel of Christ alone lies the only hope for the world by the regeneration of the individual. All else consists merely of "dead works" without permanent value before God and may be written down as "vanity".' That was a more hardline position – actually negative about social work.

When asked what the difference was between CICCU and SCM, a common reply was to the effect that, while the SCM concerned itself with the social application of Christianity, the CICCU concerned itself with Christianity itself – a personal relationship to God. As a statement of fact this was true, though it was not the whole story and perhaps it was not the best way of explaining things. In this, however, the CICCU reflected the evangelicalism of the period. At a time when few nominal Christians knew the gospel, concern with social questions seemed a fatal distraction from the main job in hand, and CICCU leaders thought that they could see that social concern had led the SCM into spiritual ineffectiveness. The CICCU perhaps overreacted to the SCM, as did evangelicals generally. The questions to be asked should have been, first, is such concern biblical? Secondly, what sort of priority does it have?

It is interesting, however, that some of the leaders in a more positive evangelical attitude to social questions in Britain came from this period in the CICCU. Sir Norman Anderson, for instance, was president in 1930–1 and Sir Frederick Catherwood was vice-president in 1944. There are others also.[62] They may not have had that attitude to social questions while they were students, but once free of the need to take a stand over against the SCM it was easier to ask in a more open way what the teaching of the Bible actually does imply for social questions.

Since 1945, as the SCM weakened, a more positive attitude ruled. The CICCU, however, has always had a problem of priorities, as does the church at large. While the CICCU was (and still is) occupied with the priority of evangelism and the nurture of new Christians who know almost nothing about the Bible, social concern always seemed a remote luxury. That is a different approach to the problem from the hardline quotation from *Old Paths* given above. The CICCU has increasingly seen social concern as right, but needing to be left very largely until one is in the real world of employment and the wider community, where the problems and opportunities are no longer armchair questions. It has never been more than a small number of members who have felt, while still students, that these questions had priority. In the 1930s it might have been looked at not only as a dangerous diversion from the task in hand but, in terms of the quotation given, as an un-biblical thing to be doing. Nevertheless, by 1970 it was perfectly accepted for some members to go to specialized conferences (mainly of graduates) where these concerns were being examined.

Before 1946 many CICCU members, when they left Cambridge, weakened their basic evangelical convictions if they got into social questions. The two had seemed in-compatible and some of the liberal leaders in Cambridge frequently said to CICCU men, 'The CICCU is fine to get you converted; but if you want to live in the real world, you must go on to another theology.' After 1946 this was no longer so persuasive. That was partly because the then CICCU members were older and as experienced in life as those who said this. And it was partly because in the late 1930s and early 1940s the foundation had already begun to be laid for a more plainly biblical theology that was not so dominated by reactions. It was now easier to ask, 'What does the Bible say and what are its applications to any and every sphere of life?' There is as yet no evangelical consen-sus, but the approach is healthier.

Chapter 8
1945–55
The renewed evangelicalism

When the war finished and the ex-servicemen came back, they provided a maturer community. Many were married, and the sight of undergraduates pushing prams was greeted with astonishment by those who had known the university in the 1930s. During the war, when an Exec member became engaged to a member of one of the London University CUs evacuated to Cambridge for the war, some assumed he would resign from the committee because he had set an undesirable example! The public-school attitude to women had predominated and some CICCU men held aloof and often rudely ignored women whom they had known in the CU when they met them elsewhere in public. A wartime Exec, after spending 24 hours discussing the possible amalgamation of the CICCU with the CWICCU, decided that, even though it was probably desirable, the male membership did not want it and it should wait until they did. The post-war generation amalgamated the two Unions in 1948 with hardly a ripple of dissent.

Evangelism was direct and outreach widespread. Undergraduates knew what evil was. Many were aware of sin in their lives, and interest in the gospel was much easier to arouse than it had been before the war. Schoolboy philosophies had been shattered in the Forces. The CICCU seized the opportunity with enthusiasm. The official religious establishment was strong and many of the college chaplains were able people. College chapels were well attended again and not all the CICCU men saw the need to give a distinctively biblical witness. Nevertheless the initiative went increasingly to men whose Christian life had stood the test of time in the Forces. On the whole that meant men whose lives had been fed on personal prayer and Bible reading. The leaders in chapel groups were therefore often sympathetic to the CICCU, if they were not actually members. The CICCU grew in size and effectiveness.

Some of the new leaders had been at Cambridge for part of a course before or during the war. The old spiritual emphases were maintained. Besides, the ex-service leaders were men of action, prepared to stand up to anyone, however academically respectable, without fear. The CICCU lost its slight inferiority complex. The theology lecturers and college tutors were, after all, not so much older and they often knew less of life than the students. Tyndale House was a help and men continued to get good theological degrees in fair numbers. The DPM and Saturday night Bible Reading grew.

The number of overseas students in Cambridge increased greatly after the war and for the first time the CICCU began to do a more adequate job in welcoming and helping them. It was never more than a small group who were greatly involved with this work and there is bound to be some regret that so few were active. The overseas students of that generation have become extremely influential leaders in many countries. Happily, there were a number of outstanding Christians among them who owe at least something to the friendship and witness of the CICCU. In the Billy Graham Mission (1955) it needed a persistent assistant missioner to persuade the CICCU to organize, at short notice, a meeting in Trinity Old Combination Room at which Dr Graham himself spoke. The CICCU thought that few would come, but over 120 turned up and the meeting had to be moved to the dining hall, for which urgent and rather irregular permission was gained at the last moment. Many were deeply impressed.

The cooperation question again

In 1946 all the Christian groups in the university were invited to join in a new unity under a body called 'Koinonia'.[63] At first the CICCU was involved, but its members soon discovered how superficial the unity was. A widespread and spontaneous feeling developed that 'the impetus of such an effort would be slight in view of the loose doctrinal basis and the varied devotional standards of its supporters'. By April 1946 the CICCU decided to plan their own Mission for February 1947 and were as certain as their predecessors that 'unity in doctrine is essential as a basis for evangelism'. So the CICCU withdrew from Koinonia, but agreed that the Mission should coincide with the Koinonia Mission. The latter had an able and well-known speaker, Alec Vidler. The CICCU, following the pattern of several not very effective previous Missions, had a team of three, each to speak for two or three nights. It did not look promising and a number of the CICCU leaders were uncertain as to whether these plans were right.

In July a small CICCU party at Keswick, including the president, heard the dramatic and effective preaching of Dr Donald Grey Barnhouse from USA. They decided to ask him to be their missioner. He could not manage February 1947, but offered November 1946 instead. After prayer the CICCU president accepted and returned to his lodgings to find a letter from Koinonia to say that they were forced to alter the date of their Mission also – by one week. The CICCU therefore, to the relief of many, went on alone again. February 1947, when the Koinonia Mission was held, also proved to be one of the coldest months on record. With a fuel shortage to match, it was an unfortunate month for a Mission. November 1946 proved far better.

The great Missions

This Mission was well planned. Wartime administrative experience was useful and, in spite of bread rationing, over 100 smaller tea meetings (squashes) were planned for the week. A substantial team of associate missioners was employed for the first time and they were kept constantly busy. Barnhouse preached in Great St Mary's (because Holy Trinity Church was too small) to packed audiences – rarely fewer than 800. Many doubters and many frank unbelievers came and heard a lively, well-illustrated and authoritative message from the Bible. Many will remember Barnhouse's dramatic description of himself as a child trying to lift himself off the ground by his own bootlaces – a comparison with justification by works.

One young atheist, a leader of the university Communist Party, was brought along. She was converted and subsequently became a missionary in Japan. Her interest had first been aroused by the life of a Christian friend who was a fellow member of the university hockey side. As so often, it was primarily Christian friendship which persuaded people to come to hear the gospel. There were many other converts, some prominent today in Christian work.

Barnhouse was exceedingly dogmatic. He did not have an after-meeting, but nevertheless preached for decision. He was scathing about contemporary theology and provoked the theological faculty to anger. One of his addresses to theological students was based on Malachi 2 in terms that were crude and far from calculated to win friends ('I will spread dung upon your faces'). He was witty, pugnacious and sincere, very good in the numerous personal interviews which he had. When he left, over 100 had professed conversion, many had been stirred up to seek further and the CICCU had finally abandoned all hesitation. It stood in a new way as an assertively evangelical body in doctrine and in evangelism.

The CICCU grew, with some college groups up to thirty strong. The weekly college Bible study and prayer meeting were well attended. The united Saturday night Bible Reading had to be moved once from the Henry Martyn Hall to a bigger hall and again, in 1951, to the debating chamber of the Union. It drew up to 350, occasionally more, and was probably the largest meeting of any kind in Cambridge on a Saturday night (the university had at that time about 8,000 members). The DPM swelled and on Sundays drew 140 or more. There was no room to kneel and insufficient time for all to take part. Prayers were brief and precise and finished with a resounding 'Amen'. There were nearly 600 at the Sunday sermon as a rule, perhaps one-third of them non-Christians.

In 1949 Barnhouse came for a second Mission. Once more God gave many striking conversions; once more there was controversy and antagonism. Barnhouse was merciless with other views including, in CICCU circles, those who did not share his pre-millennial view of the second coming. Those who felt his lash did not usually like it. But, if he was rough, it was a language the ex-service undergraduates understood, even if the smoother seniors thought it bad taste. Almost all the male students had either done war service or a two-year national service.

The November 1952 Mission was led by John Stott. Until 1950 he had been a curate in a London parish and he was still in his early thirties, though now rector of All Souls' Church in London. He had been a leading member of the CICCU during the war and understood the Cambridge scene. He was biblical, scholarly though not academic, firm though not caustic, more evidently a man with love for people than some of the older preachers. The impact was perhaps broader than any Mission since 1900. Ten years later Basil Atkinson wrote of this, 'I judge it to be the highest point of those wonderful nine years (1946–55), the nearest to revival that we have yet reached.' A very large number professed faith in Christ. The liberals began to comment on John Stott as a new phenomenon in evangelicalism and to be aware that the CICCU was not to be ignored in theology, apologetics or thoughtful evangelism. In fact the phenomenon was not new. John Stott represented the best of the CICCU tradition. The only new thing was that he was one of the younger men who had got as much as possible out of doing a modern theology course (getting a 'first'). He could speak to the theologs and others with sympathy as well as with biblical authority. His addresses formed the basis of the IVP book *Basic Christianity*.[64]

Christianity was presented as inescapably true both in theory and in practice and the lives of the CICCU and their works had to back it up. The focus was on the person and work of Christ. Cambridge was still at that time a community that gave a good deal of respect to Christian morality. Theology was in confusion but, as the liberals often said, 'We all believe in the Christian life and the Sermon on the Mount.' They went on, wrongly, to conclude therefore that what we believe does not matter much. It was only later that it was seen that the new theology led to the new morality. A missioner could therefore still rely on a certain awareness of sin and a good deal more biblical knowledge than would be true twenty-five years later. The

CICCU stood alone for totally free forgiveness through the death of the divine Christ as our substitute. Evangelism focused on these truths. Many students came up to Cambridge with some knowledge of 'the law of God'; very few of them really knew the gospel until they heard it at Cambridge.

Why Missions?

This may be the right point at which to ask why Missions have played such a big part in the history of the CICCU. There were two main reasons. First, Missions gave a unique opportunity of presenting the whole Christian message on the authority of God. In universities the tendency has been to regard religious views as merely human opinion open to debate and discussion and having no authority other than the transient opinions of the current academic fashion. The sermons, and especially the Missions, gave the opportunity to say clearly that God has spoken and to outline what he has said. There was a place for discussion to lead up to a Mission or to persuade people to come to hear preaching. There was a place for it to follow up a Mission afterwards. But the CICCU believed that, unless there is an authoritative declaration of the message as a word from God, we fail our listeners. The Missions focused this concern and made it plain that the CICCU had a message to declare.

Secondly, in the relatively circumscribed community of the university (Cambridge was not very large – even in 1977 there were only 11,300 students) a Mission can catch the ear of a large percentage of the university. Publicity, especially personal invitations, creates the situation where a large proportion of the student body can be talking about the theme of the Mission and it becomes easy to invite people to come to hear for themselves.

Missions have been of enormous importance in the

relatively residential community of Cambridge and they have played a similar role in student evangelism in many other countries. Of course, Missions have sometimes been looked to in the wrong way; CU members have expected them to be some automatic machine that produces converts. When this has been the case, the result has been unfortunate. But if Missions are looked on as a means of sowing rather than reaping – of reaching the normally unreached – then there is a logic in holding one every three years, as the CICCU has done for so long. In this way it is hoped that at least once in his or her time in Cambridge every student would have the best possible opportunity of hearing the gospel, even if he or she had no Christian friends. God mightily blessed these efforts over the years and the big Missions in that period were in their own way each a major step forward in the evangelistic outreach of the CICCU.

Billy Graham

In 1954, while Billy Graham was conducting his first big crusade in Britain at Harringay, it was suggested that he should come to Cambridge. One of the weekend speakers (Fred H. Crittenden) offered to stand down if Graham could come just for the sermon, and he agreed. Over tea with the president some remarks by Graham about the nature of the university provoked Fred Crittenden into saying that he hoped Dr Graham would preach just a simple, direct gospel address and not try to pander to the intellectual debating interests of the students. The president agreed. Graham was surprised and rose from the table saying that in that case he had to revise what he was going to say. The service proved fruitful in conversions and also in encouraging Billy Graham to emphasize direct evangelism in his student addresses. He was impressed that the Cambridge students had been willing to listen to that sort of address and had not needed academic argument.

In 1955 Billy Graham came over specially from the USA for the CICCU Mission, bringing only one or two American friends with him. He was supported by John Stott and a large team of assistant missioners. Great St Mary's was used again, as Holy Trinity was too small, and an overflow relay was arranged in Holy Trinity. Relays by landline were also arranged to other university CUs. Huge numbers attended. There was extensive counselling of enquirers, including not a few dons and research students, and many professed conversion. So extensive was the response that follow-up proved difficult. Many continued to attend Great St Mary's and a regular meeting was started by Christian dons for those seniors who had been helped. The college chaplains helped those who were interested and many who professed conversion were weaned from the evangelical tradition by encouragement to go in another direction.

The IVF and IFES

The CICCU continued to have a fairly strong link with IVF. In 1946, for instance, a new CU with six freshers was started at Leicester University College (now Leicester University). The CICCU sent a team for a long weekend and helped to launch the CU into a much more wide-ranging witness in the university. Teams were sent by arrangement with IVF to several other universities for evangelistic outreach. The CICCU also provided a good many key members of the IVF national (student) executive committee, including a high proportion of its missionary secretaries and its chairmen in the years 1945–55.

Two Oxford and two Cambridge men went together, after they had graduated, to New England to help the IVCF of USA in that area for one year, and a considerable number of young graduates took teaching posts in African universities and grammar schools. In Africa university education was developing rapidly. These graduates helped to start Scripture Union groups in schools and Christian Unions in universities and colleges. A Barnhouse Mission convert, Nigel Sylvester, became the leader of the Scripture Union work in Africa. When he came home his place was taken by John Dean, who had been converted at the CICCU freshers' sermon in 1950.

The Indian movement (the Union of Evangelical Students of India) was started by an Indian professor and a former CICCU man (David C. C. Watson) getting together to run Bible studies in the colleges and a Sunday night evening meeting in a church (echoes of the CICCU). It was remarkable that the new evangelical student movements emerging all round the world and joining the International Fellowship of Evangelical Students often had a Membership Basis that was essentially, though in their own language, 'I declare my faith in Jesus Christ as my Saviour, my Lord and my God.'

An old CICCU man, David Adeney, who had helped to start the Chinese IVF, became the associate general secretary of the IFES for the Far East and exerted a great influence for the spread of the work in that area.

The Cambridge Seventy

During most of this period missionary interest was at a low ebb. In 1951, however, Basil Atkinson spoke at a Missionary Breakfast on the missionary tradition of the CICCU. He mentioned that at one time about 40 out of a total membership of 100 members had gone abroad. Someone asked how many were committed to foreign service at that time. The missionary secretary answered that there were only 16. This was at a time when the CICCU membership was nearly 400. An ex-service freshman in the meeting, John Wheatley Price, wrote, 'That disturbed me deeply,' and it drove him to prayer. In 1954–5 he became Missionary Secretary and some time shortly before that felt challenged that God was calling the CICCU to pray not for a Cambridge Seven but for a Cambridge Seventy. He and others were suspicious of this sort of thing, but gradually the idea took root. The challenge was presented to the CICCU in the spring term of 1955 and during the following year an informal roll was kept of those who committed themselves to foreign missionary service. The prayer was 'That seventy of our generation in the CICCU should serve the Lord overseas.' Some who pledged themselves to go in fact never went; and others who joined in the prayer letter which was circulated for many years never committed themselves to going. In the end over sixty (almost if not quite seventy) did go abroad. Missionary prayer groups were also developed again and were active still over twenty years later.

It cannot be said that this constituted a revival of missionary concern, but a substantial proportion of that generation of CICCU members went abroad, particularly when there was such a strong call to the home ministry as well. The Seventy also provided everyone with a challenge to self-sacrificing service.

The college chapels

The CICCU had learnt the necessity of being distinct from the college chapels.[65] The preliminaries of the Billy Graham Mission provoked an interesting and representative conflict with them. The CICCU had as usual gone ahead and appointed college assistant missioners without consultation with the religious authorities. The latter, however, found themselves in a new and slightly difficult position. For the first time the CICCU was at least as large and probably more influential at the undergraduate level than the chapels. Although the CICCU had been firm and gracious, the chaplains naturally wanted to be in on what they could see would be the major Christian activity of the year. The deans and chaplains, who had a regular meeting in which only a few were sympathetic to the CICCU, started a correspondence with the CICCU Exec over the question of follow-up of the forthcoming mission. In one letter they wrote that they had obtained the agreement of the Bishop of Ely for Billy Graham (a Baptist) to preach in Great St Mary's on the condition that all names of converts were given to the college chaplains. This was unacceptable to the CICCU and there was thought of moving the Mission to some other more neutral meeting-place, if one could be found at short notice. The deans and chaplains were warned by the sympathetic few among their number that they had made an almost impossible demand. The CICCU Exec consulted friends in the IVF and elsewhere, who all advised standing firm. While they tried to work out an answer, the correspondence with the chaplains continued on other topics. After a while the CICCU replied that they noted that the question of converts' names had now been dropped. They hoped it could be forgotten. To associate the CICCU so closely with the chaplains in this way, they said, would imply a degree of unity in doctrine that neither the CICCU nor the chaplains really wished to maintain. The subject was never raised again. The Mission was held in Great St Mary's, and the CICCU did not give names to the chaplains.

Probably the CICCU was never stronger than it was in that period. The membership, which rose to 400, consisted of students who for the most part understood what the CICCU was for and why it gave a distinctive witness. Many who had been converted in Cambridge continued afterwards in effective Christian witness. The CICCU was not as large as it has sometimes been since, but it was more clearly defined as a biblical group than it sometimes became when it grew much larger. The rediscovery of evangelical truth as the power of God for conversion and for spiritual life was fresh and exciting. Of course, for each generation it is a fresh discovery. But there was little danger of regarding the preaching of the gospel as dull or too 'traditional', as was sometimes the case later. There was no desire to do and say things differently just for the sake of being different, and hardly any of the negative attitudes to doctrine that developed in some college groups in the late 1960s and 1970s.

Of course, rebels could still go off and join the SCM, and some did so, but to belong to the CICCU was counted both a privilege and a responsibility. It made members realize the necessity of consistency of thought and life, because the rest of the university was watching to see whether a Bible-based Christianity might after all be the answer to the theological wilderness or to the personal sense of emptiness that was common.

A small survey done on those who had been CICCU members in one college in 1950 showed that all were active Christians ten years later. There had probably been some 'casualties' among those who professed conversion, but who never joined the CU. Those who got as far as joining, however, had continued consistently.

CICCU members met sufficient criticism to keep them aware that they were a city set on a hill that could not be hid. It was fairly obvious that no other substantial group was offering men and women a genuine salvation. The next fifteen years were not quite so clear cut.

To quote Basil Atkinson again, 'The CICCU was the largest of all University Societies except the Union Society. It had the respect of the University and was recognized as the leading religious society. Thousands of undergraduates heard the gospel during those wonderful years. Hundreds were converted and are in the world somewhere today serving the Master. The CICCU was no longer on the defensive. Its message was recognized by many as the genuine truth. There was a positive note of power and of aggressive evangelism.'[66]

Chapter 9

1955–77

Defence and proclamation

As the CICCU moved into and beyond the mid-1950s, it continued to live with elements of controversy – in this case, what became known as 'the fundamentalist controversy'.

The fundamentalist controversy

The news that Billy Graham was going to lead the CICCU Mission sparked off a public debate in the correspondence columns of *The Times*. Canon Luce of Durham started it by writing in August 1955, 'The recent increase of fundamentalism among university students cannot but cause concern to those whose work lies in religious education. No branch of education can make terms with an outlook which ignores the conclusions of modern scholarship in that particular department of knowledge. In this connection the proposal that Dr Graham should conduct a mission to Cambridge University raises an issue which does not seem to have been squarely faced by Christians in this country. Universities exist for the advancement of learning; on what basis, therefore, can fundamentalism claim a hearing at Cambridge?' The vicar of Great St Mary's and the Regius Professor of Divinity at Cambridge signed a joint reply to say, in effect, that it was not their fault: 'The mission is a private venture, and does not commit the university, or the Church in the university.' Basil Atkinson, in a typically succinct letter, replied 'as one who is proud to be taking a small part in the preparation for Dr Graham's proposed mission'. 'The gospel preached by Dr Graham', he wrote, 'is in accord with true scholarship illuminated by revelation. It originates in the New Testament . . . and it will still be preached when the modernistic concepts of today have been superseded and discarded.' An assistant bishop wrote in support of Dr Graham. The Bishop of Durham and several others, some of them the old stalwarts of liberalism, wrote against him. G. T. Manley and John Stott and a recent convert from Dr Graham's Harringay crusade joined in. A layman pointedly asked, 'Have your right reverend and reverend correspondents who are opposed to fundamentalism forgotten that at their own ordination they solemnly and publicly declared that they "unfeignedly believed all the canonical scriptures of the Old and New Testament"?'[67]

The controversy continued for some time in other circles. In 1956 two bishops wrote anti-fundamentalist articles in diocesan papers. The most vigorous, and in many ways the most unexpected, was that of the Bishop of Durham, A. M. Ramsey. He had just been nominated Archbishop of York and later became Archbishop of Canterbury. In an article on 'The Menace of Fundamentalism' he mentioned Billy Graham and the IVF, offered a caricature of an evangelistic meeting (presumably from second-hand reports), and then wrote, 'He (Billy Graham) has gone. Our English fundamentalism remains. It is *heretical* . . . It is *sectarian* . . . The church must pray that men will be raised up with the power so to preach, that the stream of conversions will not be followed by a backwash of moral casualties and disillusioned sceptics.'[68]

What surprised people was that Ramsey was not particularly liberal, but a relatively conservative High Churchman. His theological lectures in Cambridge, where he had shortly before been a theology professor, had been appreciated by CICCU members as some of the most constructive and orthodox of the whole faculty. The CICCU had even suggested to the Durham University CU that, when Ramsey went there as Bishop, he might be willing to chair a meeting of the CU Mission. Ramsey knew quite well, however, that the High Church message was not the same as that of the CICCU. It emerged that he was relatively conservative not so much because of the teaching of the Bible, but rather because of the teaching of the church, that he did not share the CICCU's emphasis on personal faith and new birth and was very unhappy about the emphasis on substitutionary atonement and the final authority and infallibility of the Bible.

It is probably significant that Ramsey had been the student chairman of the introductory meeting of the Willy Nicholson Mission in 1926 (see p. 103 above). Ramsey had then been president of the Union Society. Perhaps he still thought in terms of the reputation of Willy Nicholson. Almost certainly he had been badly briefed by men far more hostile than himself. The fact was that the CICCU members were some of the very few who actually believed in the official doctrines of the Church of England as expressed in the Thirty-nine Articles. For Anglicans who were at all liberal to call the CICCU heretical was rather ridiculous. The innuendo of Ramsey's last sentence about moral casualties was without foundation.

In 1957 the High Churchman Gabriel Hebert wrote a

book which was a more systematic attack. This was entitled *Fundamentalism and the Church of God* (SCM Press, 1957). Hebert attacked conservative evangelicals for their doctrine of Scripture and for their view of the church and its sacraments. This provoked a reply by J. I. Packer in his book *'Fundamentalism' and the Word of God* (IVP, 1958), which has provided the greatest possible help to many generations of students, not least in the CICCU. It set out clearly and logically the classic, historic view of Scripture as the Word of God. Packer explained what this did and did not mean (over against caricatures), defending it against misrepresentation and attacks, and showing that the church could not stand on any other foundation.

It is significant that the High Church leaders were as worried as the more consistently liberal leaders by the re-emergence of evangelicalism.[69] For the most part they were also mildly liberal in their attitude to the Bible, but they were not rationalists. They believed what they believed because it was the teaching of their church; a theology ruled by evangelical principles – by the death of Christ alone, by faith alone, by the Word of God alone – was no more palatable to most of them than it was to the liberals. Anti-fundamentalism became a popular pastime for a number of years. Rude remarks about Billy Graham or fundamentalists seemed a sure way of rousing support for speakers in many different kinds of meetings. The High Church theologians had been drawn in partly because they were more theologically minded than most of the liberals, but the backbone of the attack was from a more rationalistic standpoint, as Canon Luce's original letter illustrated.

This was by no means the last that was heard of old-fashioned liberal opposition. It represented the defiant shouts of those who had perhaps begun to realize that the Christian world was turning full circle. Liberalism, which had been launched with such high hopes that it would reach the intelligent unchurched people, had proved a failure in that respect. Meanwhile the supposedly anti-intellectual evangelicals were recapturing the minds of intelligent and educated young people as well as of the uneducated. This was happening in a way that confounded their critics. Their protest was the despairing cry of those who could do nothing to stop the tide but who sincerely believed it to be a major disaster.

High Church leaders such as Ramsey and Hebert also saw their own party in the church beginning to decline and the evangelicals gaining an increasing percentage of ordinands for the Church of England. As the Bishop of Southwell (F. R. Barry) said in a speech in the Convocation of York, 'It was a pretty serious business for the Church of England if any very considerable or increasing proportion of its ministry was going to be recruited with an outlook and an approach of that kind.'[70] There were similarities to the feelings of the conservative evangelicals in the parishes when liberalism seemed to be carrying all before it in the universities in the 1900–25 period. In this case, however, the old guard (liberal and High Church) was overwhelmingly strong in the teaching and preaching posts in the universities. Nevertheless, they could not persuade the students. The 1955 generation of evangelicals largely ignored what the liberals were saying and set about trying to rebuild student witness (and, when they went down from university, church life) on biblical foundations. A few of the more scholarly men among them read the current theology carefully, obtained first-class degrees and postgraduate qualifications, and tried to start rebuilding an evangelical theology.

A new situation

In many ways the Stott Mission of 1952 was the climax,

but the Billy Graham Mission of 1955 and the second Stott Mission in 1958 carried on the work. Both created opposition, as was inevitable. Stott gave less offence because he was harder to dismiss in the university. No-one could deny his right to be heard and what he said had to be reckoned with as an exposition of New Testament Christianity. Graham could be more easily dismissed as 'an American Revivalist' and his stronger pressure for decision was an obvious target of criticism by some.

In 1958 John Stott came again for a Mission under the title 'What think ye of Christ?' The title may sound quaint in the twenty-first century, but was appropriate then. Every college had its own assistant missioner and the CICCU gathered together on the team a remarkable group of young evangelical ministers and laymen. Such a team could not have been found ten years before. Many of them were the fruits of the evangelism and teaching in the CICCU and OICCU during the previous fifteen years. They brought to light one important side-effect of the evangelistic preaching and the Missions of these years. A growing number of students had received a call to the ministry and a major factor in this had been that they had been given a new vision for a preaching ministry. In this the examples of John Stott and Dr Martyn Lloyd-Jones in London had probably played a key part. The ministry was seen in a new way as an opportunity to preach the Word of God with the authority of God. Evangelical theological colleges, especially in the Church of England, had begun to fill up again and to expand with numerous young graduates, including many who had been converted in the CICCU and the OICCU since the war. Churches long in the hands of those with other outlooks began to be recaptured for a more biblical ministry. The principal of Ridley Hall (a liberal evangelical) lamented that the impetus had gone out of the liberal evangelical tradition and that nearly all the men coming to Ridley were now from a conservative evangelical background with experience in the evangelical youth movements or in the university CUs. No-one could seriously doubt that the evangelical movement was gaining ground fairly rapidly, and this was obvious so as far as Cambridge was concerned.

A new situation therefore arose in the late 1950s. For decades the other religious groups had regarded the CICCU as an almost negligible sideshow on the religious scene. They now woke up to the fact that it was the largest and most lively force at the undergraduate level. It could not be ignored. For example, if its members did not attend a chapel (they usually did in fair numbers), the chapel would often be relatively empty. However far removed they were theologically, a growing number of chaplains began to be more friendly in their attitude towards the CICCU.

By 1955 the SCM was declining and even the denominational societies, which had had a short revival, had mostly reached, and in some cases already passed, a peak from which they steadily fell away.[71] The ex-war-service generation was finishing. The new students were younger and less religious. Humanism began to gain ground. For an increasing number of students it was a choice between no religion at all or an out-and-out religion which was not afraid to be definite about the faith. Some CICCU college freshers' squashes changed from a bland, familiar theme, such as 'Christianity in University Life', to themes such as 'God has spoken'. Freshers' evangelism was very important. Every college had a meeting at which the elements of the gospel were explained. Many whose interest was aroused then went on to become Christians at the freshers' sermon or later in the first term. Most of those converted in this period were probably first-year students.

The CICCU brought up a very strong team of speakers

for these freshers' squashes each year and made this outreach a major effort. But gradually the emphasis on the freshers' squashes as an initial evangelistic outreach declined. By 1965 most colleges had lapsed into a meeting at which CU members talked harmlessly about the activities of the CICCU – until some older members urged that the opportunity be not missed. The defence was that they wanted to show that the CICCU was human – something, it might be thought, that was hardly in doubt. Nevertheless, some freshers' squashes had perhaps sometimes been too aggressive. But to the extent that change came in, it represented a weakening of the ideal of the CICCU as essentially a witness – an evangelistic body rather than just a fellowship. It was not until around 1970 that the situation was restored.

The 1960s

The CICCU has not always gone on from strength to strength. It is difficult to be certain why the 1960s were a disappointing period. A good solid work was still done. The evangelistic ideal was by no means lost and, compared with most other bodies, it was very fruitful. It became accepted that at least a third of the members (it had probably been over a half in the 1950s) had become personal Christians since coming up. When there were hopes for striking advances, however, they did not come until a new surge of life made itself felt in 1969–71.

There is no doubt that the university became more hostile to Christian influences in the 1960s. In 1960 the college chapels were well attended; by 1967 they were relatively empty. The DPM correspondingly declined from 40 or 50 in 1960, with 100-plus on Sundays, to a very low ebb by 1967. Sometimes the numbers were in single figures. The CICCU Sunday night evangelistic sermon attendance also declined. There was talk of discontinuing both the DPM and the sermons, and there was uncertainty among the leaders. The new generation of students seemed to be a touch more careless and more conceited. It was not so easy to get a good audience and the CICCU members had to work harder to bring their friends. The Mission in 1961 (led by Kenneth Prior) was hard going and numbers built up only slowly. But God blessed once more and quite a few became Christians during that time and went on to active Christian life and witness. When attendance at the DPM was made a major topic for prayer, it gradually recovered.

The CICCU also faced some new internal problems. For instance, a very strongly Calvinistic group emerged around 1960. At first it led to a sharp polarization: people were either ardently for it or strongly against it. Because its criticism of CICCU traditions concentrated on the methods and content of evangelism, it left some members too uncertain of themselves to get on with the job. It was argued, for instance, that Revelation 3:20, which had been a favourite evangelistic verse for many, should not be used in evangelism. Even John 3:16 came under fire as a text for this purpose. At first the CICCU Exec overreacted a little, but then, partly with the sane advice of Basil Atkinson and others, allowed the conflict to blow itself out. The more Calvinistic brought with them a very helpful emphasis on biblical doctrine and on the value of some of the older Puritans and similar more recent books. When the polarization died down all were able to work together again with mutual benefit.

As has frequently happened elsewhere, the strong Calvinistic influence was followed by a swing to a charismatic influence. At first the CICCU leadership reacted even more strongly to this, especially as it derived from independent visiting speakers who set up their own groups in some colleges. The charismatics tended to regard the doctrinal emphasis of the more Calvinistic and the debates it had engendered as highly unprofitable. The CICCU leaders feared that the charismatic groups would lead to so much concentration on fellowship and self-concern that the evangelistic thrust would be lost. They had feared the same result from the Calvinistic influence. Both these emphases were really new in the CICCU. It had been mildly 'Reformed' all along, with its emphasis on grace, and it had stressed the work of the Holy Spirit along Keswick lines. But it had not included any appreciable number of strong representatives of either emphasis before.[72]

Whatever the reasons, the 1960s did see the CICCU more taken up with internal problems. It became all too easy for Christian freshers to be so smothered with Christian friendship that when they had found their feet at the end of the first term they had few non-Christian friends. The responsibility to be a soul-winner was not so obviously laid on all the members. This had one advantage in that the less extrovert people felt more at home in the CU, but it also meant that there was a certain loss of vision for the CICCU as primarily an agency for witness to non-Christians.

Arts faculty witness

Another change came on that was entirely for the good. During the Second World War the CICCU had overwhelmingly consisted of scientists, engineers and medicals; no-one else much was able to stay for more than six or twelve months, because of the conscription. This emphasis continued to a considerable extent after the war. In the 1960s a growing proportion of students in the arts faculties came into the CU and this was not at first so easy to cope with. These members wanted to develop activities for arts students and there was relatively little senior help or even good literature to guide them. Between the wars the bigger apologetic debates had seemed to be on the science and religion question and some evangelical literature on these aspects had been published. By the 1960s there was an excellent group of professors of science and medicine available to speak.

There was hardly a single evangelical professor (and very few lecturers) in the fields of history, literature, languages, economics, politics or philosophy. Evangelical students in these fields began to discover that the apologetic questions were as important here as anywhere else, and the CICCU began to branch out in its concerns. A successful visit by Professor Rookmaaker (Professor of the History of Art at the Free University, Amsterdam) was arranged by the Exec in 1969 and surprised some people by the number of students it attracted and interested. By the 1970s excellent groups were working in several of these fields. Some groups produced plays and other activities to try to reach their section of the university better. There was healthy debate about the scope of such things, but no-one was now criticized for having an interest in contemporary culture.

Apologetics

The 1971 Mission was led by Michael Green and included pre-Mission activities on a new scale, to reach every section of the university. Eighty musicians, for instance, came to a special meeting for that department. The magazine *Really*, which started in 1968 and became established about 1970, was an unofficial effort to reach out and was often highly effective. By this time it was a matter of course for CICCU members to be interested in the application of biblical truth to their academic field, whatever it was, whereas such a concern had been unusual in the 1940s and even rather suspect in the 1920s.

Over the same period the style of some of the central evangelistic activities began to change. In the late 1950s a series of apologetic addresses was launched, again on mid-week evenings. This time they were much more successful and were well attended. They did not altogether please those who felt that the CU should keep to 'the simple gospel'. Significantly, there were few old CICCU men available as speakers. Most of those who came to speak were from other universities where the Christians, as students or research students, had been pushed more vigorously into debate. Almost immediately it became clear that these lectures would reach some who did not go to church and did not come to CICCU sermons. The knowledge that one or two had gone on to attend CICCU sermons and been converted was a great encouragement.

By 1970 an experiment was carried out in holding two lectures a term on a Sunday night in the Senate House. These were in the place of the sermon which had been held weekly, usually in Holy Trinity Church, since the 1920s. The aim was to reach the less religious who would not easily come into a church and for whom Sunday night was nevertheless far more likely to be free than a week night. These lectures continued irregularly and undoubtedly reached new people, often drawing in far more students than the sermons, though inevitably giving a less solid biblical content because the speakers had to keep to their subjects. This was not a substitute for proclamation, but a preparation, and conversions came in personal talks after these lectures. Nevertheless, the Sunday-night (8.30pm) sermons, by then called 'addresses', remained a main means of evangelism and every member was encouraged to bring a friend. From this point on, however, they were not held every week. The occasional Sunday was left free for the lectures or for college-based evangelism arranged independently by each college group.

Meanwhile, the theological pressures, if less extreme than before, seemed just as strong. A large number of

CICCU members read theology, sometimes constituting a high proportion of the faculty. By no means all could stand up to the constant pressure to move away from a conservative evangelical position and the CICCU lost a steady trickle of members because their studies drew them to another outlook. This problem was nothing like as serious as it had been in the 1930s, partly because there was more help. The Theological Students' Fellowship of the IVF, for instance, promoted literature, conferences and speakers. It was also partly because the members had not started from such an extreme position themselves and therefore could appreciate some good in the course without feeling threatened.

A weaker period

To go back a little, the period 1965–9 was a relatively low point in the post-Second World War period. Outwardly the CICCU had strong numbers and it was still doing good work, but it had lost some of its vigour. The sheer size of the CU – now about 400 – forced the college groups to take the main load of fellowship and evangelism. Some colleges had their own DPM. The Exec were torn between the desire to encourage groups at the college level and the desire to maintain a stronger central fellowship and witness. There was a short period when a good many (including some of the Exec) were all for reducing central activities to a minimum.

In 1968 a group of college reps wrote to all the members criticizing the central programme, including the DPM. That was the turning point and members began once more to see that such united activities were important. DPM numbers increased again and support for sermons improved when the alternatives were faced. In fact, the DPM increased from the day that people met to pray about the possibility of discontinuing it! In January 1970 an excellent preterminal house party, with a great spirit of prayer, marked the change. The general committee (i.e. college reps) voted overwhelmingly to continue the DPM.[73]

From this discussion the CU emerged with an emphasis on the college group as a means of fellowship and Bible study, but with renewed emphasis on the DPM and on other central activities for teaching (Saturday Bible Readings) and evangelism (the Sunday sermons and lectures).

The 1970s

During the 1970s the CICCU grew considerably. Undoubtedly students became more interested in religion. As one Christian fresher remarked, 'Almost everyone is willing to talk seriously about Christian things if given the opportunity.' A large 'fringe' of the kind of people who, in the 1930s, would have been out of earshot of the CICCU and busy in SCM or the chapel, were now fairly frequent attenders, though not usually members. Such a 'fringe' offered enormous possibilities and represented an opportunity on a new scale. Many of those who now came to the CICCU had never been evangelicals and only gradually or partially came to an evangelical standpoint as they studied the Bible or listened to Bible Readings and sermons. The result was that the CICCU was a little less clearly defined and there were rather more people within its circle who were not so content with the strong and consistently evangelical programme.

The freshers' programme had revived by 1970 and, apart from the primary function of reaching freshers, it often served to unite the college groups, which were now increasingly called 'College CUs'. As one rep in a somewhat divided college wrote, 'To have a definite aim (the freshers' work) really caused the group to come together in fellowship in a natural way (rather than introspective).

Prayer meetings were full of prayer and expectancy! Instead of "we are going to enjoy warm fellowship", suddenly we had common prayer needs and concerns, which welded the group together.'

The freshers' outreach was something that all the second- and third-year members did together and it set a pattern for the year. In this period, also, many college CUs started holding their own house parties – perhaps with one or two other colleges. But after the uncertainty of the 1960s, the DPM, sermons, missions and Saturday night Bible Readings were strengthened again. Missionary activities were also continued on a united basis and the college reps realized afresh the value of the wider fellowship of the CICCU and their official links with an Exec member.

There was renewed growth and the Missions of 1971 and 1974 played a substantial part in this. Both were marked by good attendances (up to 1,000 each night) and large numbers professing conversion. There was an increasing flow of Christian freshers, with a considerable sprinkling of those who had been abroad in missionary situations or similar service overseas between leaving school and going to university. They came up with rather more experience and maturity than the average Christian student and played an active and effective part in personal evangelism from the very start. The number of those professing conversion increased again, so that half the members were fairly new Christians.

By 1977 the CICCU found itself strong numerically. The formal membership was up to around 450, but perhaps twice that number or more were in Bible study groups every week. The DPM was not large on most days, but could reach 100 on Saturdays to pray for the weekend. In many colleges the prayer life was strong. Evangelistic Bible studies – special groups consisting usually of two Christians and four to six non-Christians meeting for weekly study – were a feature, in addition to the usual college group Bible studies. These represented a sign of the times, in that to so many freshers the Bible was almost unknown – and therefore interesting. These proved a major means of evangelism and many who professed conversion had been attending them or the regular Bible studies for some time. More of those professing conversion were second- or third-year students; this was perhaps because, being almost without Christian background, they needed longer to understand the message.

Some college groups had up to seventy members. This was too large to meet together in college rooms and therefore they divided up into numerous Bible study groups. In many colleges the CICCU members between them knew almost everyone in the college. In a survey in 1976, before the Mission of 1977, it was not difficult to allocate responsibility for inviting every student; even in the largest colleges, nearly every student was known personally by a CU member. Whether they also understood the gospel is another question – hence the Mission and its attempt to reach out to the whole university. But the 'coverage' was there if members were willing to use the opportunities effectively. It was constantly heard from those who professed conversion that their interest and concern were aroused by what they saw in the lives of their Christian friends. Clearly the effective witness of the CU could have been very much larger with this enormous range of personal contacts.

In this period there were too few churches or other local Christian groups around the country that drew in 300 or so young people every year and each year sent out an equal number to scatter all over the world for Christ. Having said that, however, the CICCU needed to ask why it should not double that number each year in the very favoured circumstances of their residential community.

Chapter 10
1977–2002
The gospel in changing times

In the years 1977–2002 the CICCU had continually to think through how to communicate its unchanging message in the changing student scene.[74] What were the main pressures on a continuing Christian witness in the colleges? And how did they bear on a Christian arriving at Cambridge for his or her first term?

Starting out

Christian freshers became increasingly aware of pressures from at least two sources: from outside – from the general student culture that reflected the state of society at large; and from within Christian culture too. They found that many factors in the culture of the 1980s and 1990s were against the clear expression of any firm conviction, whether by a group or an individual.

They soon met, if they did not know them already, the fashionable buzzwords of a politically correct (PC) generation, such as pluralism and tolerance. Such young Christians obviously recognized the existence of different faith communities and supported religious liberty for all.

Pluralism as a fact was one thing, but pluralism as a belief was another thing. As Christians they could not accept that the many different faith paths were equally valid, not least because the paths led in so many different directions.

Similarly, they met arguments for tolerance that were intolerant of every absolute claim – except absolute intolerance for Christianity. They probably found, to take two examples from this period, that gay rights and lifestyle were PC and beyond criticism, but that Christianity's truth claims were not.

Some found postmodern denials of absolute truth in general, and of any objective meaning in texts, coming out in lectures or set books; such views, by extension, evacuated the Bible of a given meaning. They saw that formidable intellectual barriers stood in the way of continuing a clear witness to Christ. Moreover, these barriers seemed particularly hard to shift; in an intellectual climate so dismissive of truth claims there was no point in engaging them in reasoned debate. As truth did not exist, no-one needed to give thought or answer to it. It was to be ignored, not rebutted. Christian freshers certainly had a lot to think about.

Ethics and lifestyles

These same trends affected students' ethics and lifestyles. Earlier generations had paid lip-service to inherited moral values, even if they had not lived by them; to their successors tolerance validated whatever behaviour or lifestyle they chose. 'Anything goes' was effectively the ethic; the test of acceptability was no moral code, but what satisfaction an experience might yield, or what benefit it could offer to each self. Many claimed freedom to believe and live according to choice, with self-fulfilment the one self-evident absolute. Christian first-years found that, if Christianity's truth claims were counter-cultural, its ethical stance was often offensive. In that setting young Christians quickly had to develop both intellectual convictions and moral courage in order to stand firm.

Other factors were on freshers' minds as well, such as social pressures. The switch to mixed colleges became the unquestioned norm and no longer a novelty, but that posed different questions from earlier days. As with others of their generation, more students came from unsettled or broken family backgrounds and this affected their own relationships, trust and inner security. At another level the academic pressures steadily intensified. No longer could many swan through three years while majoring on sport or pleasures. If it was tough to gain entry, it was increasingly imperative to get a good degree.

Challenges to the CICCU

These challenges had new elements, stimulating the CICCU to keep reviewing how it could hold and proclaim truth. How could it gain entry for the gospel into students' increasingly crowded lives? How could its witness continue to be biblical in content and at the same time appropriate to the changing culture? How could its apologetics engage both modern and postmodern views? Indeed, were apologetics at all relevant to postmoderns? What style of events or programme would be most helpful to get the biblical gospel across? Should proclamation still have the prime place in evangelism? How could the confrontational call of the gospel for repentance be presented?

These were pressing questions in a period when claims about absolute truth or Jesus as the only way to God were seen as power games, an infringement of others' identity or integrity. These issues faced the CICCU when it looked out on the world of its non-Christian friends and tried to understand and reach them.

Inroads of culture

At the same time as facing these challenges to evangelism, the CICCU had to deal with other factors from within Christian circles. Increasingly, Christian freshers arrived relatively illiterate biblically and with a poor grasp of the great truths of the Christian faith. Generally this was not their fault, since many had become Christians only in the year or two before starting at Cambridge and few had had the chance to receive systematic Bible teaching. With little Christian background compared to earlier generations, some seemed to have no clear understanding of why Christ died or of what he achieved on the cross.

This situation reflected the unnoticed inroads of the surrounding culture into the outlook and practice among Christians. There were many glorious exceptions to this generalization, of course. Nevertheless, many students lacked not only a firm basis for their own faith, but also the vision or knowledge to pass the gospel on to their friends.

The secular buzzwords of pluralism and tolerance had faint echoes in Christian circles. An increasingly diverse evangelical world developed a growing belief in 'unity in diversity'. In this later period this was partly the result of the increasing evangelical numbers and profile in the country at large. With the resulting greater self-confidence, interest grew in developing a theology of diversity, that would legitimize each evangelical group's freedom to express its own distinctives, even when those were not gospel truths but only the factors that denominated one group from another. This certainly succeeded in emphasizing diversity, though how it promoted unity in and love for the gospel was not so clear. These trends caused considerable difficulties for student witness in Cambridge. To some, all this suggested parallels with what happened when the

Student Christian Movement moved away from its gospel focus towards broader views.

As differences between evangelicals became more noticeable, they tended to obscure the distinction between 'the main thing' and less important things, between primary and secondary truths. So how could the CICCU continue to express unity in the gospel, in the truths 'of first importance' (1 Corinthians 15:3–4)? Indeed, what of the distinction between gospel essentials and points of difference between evangelicals: was that primary–secondary distinction still valid? And if so, how could the CICCU keep secondary things secondary, when some believed that their own distinctives were non-negotiable? Successive generations of CICCU members had to go back to Scripture on issues that affected evangelism and unity in the gospel.

How then did the CICCU fare in these twenty-five years? The basic answer is that it survived – how many organizations survive 125 changes of leadership in as many years? CICCU was still there, still alive, still seeking to live by biblical priorities. Mere survival, of course, was not the aim, but some other societies did not survive. The continued existence of the CICCU was worthy of note in view of the odds against it.

Movements come and go

Student societies, secular or religious, can appear and disappear under the impact of changing trends. The later history of the Student Christian Movement illustrates how a dominant force could dwindle and fade, as did its parent body, the World Student Christian Federation.

The General Secretary of the WSCF 1968–1972, Risto Lehtonen, provided an authoritative insider's account of what happened. In 1998 he wrote *Story of a Storm* to describe the 'socio-political storm of massive ferocity that struck the student movement of the Christian churches with results devastating and lasting'. Many factors gave rise to 'intense soul-searching in WSCF circles, seeking both a new form of the Christian message and a new strategy for reaching the student generation. Christian "presence" rather than Christian mission became the focus. Witness to Christ found its authenticity not in words or truth claims, but in terms of solidarity with the world. This story is a cautionary tale for all who care about the church in mission. We shall have to build again that evangelical confidence which only sinners continually judged and transformed by grace can know.'

Lehtonen's 'final remarks' were these: 'The continuing weakness of the worldwide ecumenical student ministry is a cause for concern. There is still nothing equivalent to a functioning SCM in Britain and in the Netherlands. Similar weakness prevails in many other parts of the world. The vacuum is very real. It can be expected that in the next phase of the ecumenical movement, religious issues will return to centre stage and that the reduction of faith to the likeness of social and political ideologies will recede.'[75]

One consequence of the demise of the SCM was that the CICCU, as generally the largest university Christian society, at times developed a bigger fringe around its formal membership than in the days when SCM was strong. That accentuated the temptations towards unity in diversity that could weaken its gospel distinctiveness. It sometimes made it harder to keep the focus clear.

Regular Missions

In this context the CICCU continued its tradition of holding weeklong Missions to the university every three years. John Stott led one entitled 'Who's Jesus?' in the CICCU's centenary year. Billy Graham followed him in 1980, twenty-five years after his first much-publicized and

much-criticized Mission. Then came Missions led by
Dick Lucas, David Jackman, John Chapman, Hugh
Palmer, Nigel Lee, Paul Weston and, in February 2001,
Rico Tice.

In the years between these main events came various
'mini-Missions', though in due course they lost the 'mini'
tag that seemed to downgrade them. The Missions all gave
prominence to proclamation or teaching evangelism, but
many other apologetic or introductory events preceded,
supported or followed them up. CICCU members' friendships in their colleges, faculties, clubs and societies were
the basis of all these.

At John Stott's 1977 Mission the Guildhall was full
every night. Three years later the Billy Graham Mission,
with even larger numbers expected, took place in the university church, Great St Mary's, but not before some issues
had had to be discussed and resolved. The CICCU at one
stage considered withdrawing from the venue, as it seemed
that its use might be conditional on passing the names of
contacts to the college deans and chaplains. For pastoral
and doctrinal reasons the CICCU was unwilling to do this
and even contemplated a marquee – in November! In the
end it did not have to seek another venue. An average of
1,850 students attended the talks every night, out of
11,000 undergraduate members of the university. With
those numbers, and many responding, the Mission needed
the large team of assistant missioners working in each
college.

The Mission also had the anticipated wide press coverage, part of which focused on the fact that Dr Graham was
staying at the Garden House Hotel, not the cheapest in
Cambridge. The minutes mentioned the threat of bomb
scares and apparently that hotel was the only one with
adequate security.

Opening up the gospel

Succeeding Missions continued to give priority to opening up the gospel, as in the one David Jackman led in 1986. The then president was 'a little disappointed after the first night of the mission. There were very few jokes or brilliant stories – just faithful exposition of John's Gospel. But people kept coming and many were converted. I still bump into people who came to faith that week – they have lasted the course. David's faithful, simple expository style was a model I have tried to copy in missions I have led. He manifestly relied not on the power of personality, but on God's Spirit at work through the Word – and God blessed that. A huge number of new Christians resulted – 100 or so.'

For all the Missions arresting and inventive publicity prepared the way for the proclamation and generally got university-wide attention. Designs, titles and the form of the meetings themselves evolved over the years in order to relate to student culture. The 'appeal' at Missions also changed. In days when most students could probably have answered a basic Bible knowledge question on *University Challenge*, it was appropriate to seek a response directly after the gospel had been explained. Missions had been seen as including definite times of reaping. But as cultural changes left more and more students knowing less and less about the faith (zero in some cases), Missions became part of a much longer and more gradual year-on-year work of preparing and sowing.

The gospel through friendship

A 1997 student commented on the growth of a biblically illiterate mindset in both non-Christian and Christian Cambridge. With students increasingly ignorant of any true idea of God, Christians wanted to find ways to dispel that ignorance. One initiative was conceived within the

Christian Union movement (the Universities and Colleges Christian Fellowship). The basic idea was to take one of the Gospels and present it in a design and format (for example, to look like a CD) that would give it immediate visual acceptance with students. Then the main aims were, first, to help all CU members to become thoroughly conversant with the gospel in the Gospel, which involved providing resources and training in Bible study; second, to encourage them to give a copy to each of their friends on a personal basis; and third, for CU members to invite these friends to come with them to a Discovering Christianity (DC) course or equivalent, which would go through the Gospel in four or six weekly sessions.

The Bible Society gave 450,000 copies of the Gospel to the whole Christian Union movement for each of the first two Gospel projects and the Scripture Gift Mission generously did the same for the third. The first was in 1994–5 with Luke's Gospel and 'The Big Idea' as the project title; 'Breakthrough' followed with John's Gospel in 1997–8; and 'Identity' with Mark in 2000–1. Each time the CICCU put its share of copies to good use. The designs for each of these won great acclaim from Christian and secular sources (not least in art colleges) and definitely helped to get students reading a Gospel. For many in post-Christian Britain this was the first time in their lives that they had ever opened a Gospel.

'The Big Idea' coincided with the CICCU 'Eternity' Mission for 1995 in the Guildhall with Nigel Lee, when the Mission talks – as well as preparation and follow-up – were based on Luke. The combination of God's Word and personal friendships was self-evidently biblical as a pattern for evangelism. This pattern also meant that, within the Mission meetings, apologetic questions arose from the teaching and claims of the Gospel, rather than being tackled as separate issues.

Nailing colours to the mast

The Paradigm Shift (pS) Mission with Paul Weston in Great St Mary's in 1998 took John's Gospel and used the CICCU's weekly Bible Readings to introduce students to that Gospel. Just before the pS Mission, the CICCU college representatives reported to the Mission Committee the number of Christians who were prepared to give out Gospels and invite friends to the talks. With only 250 signed-up CICCU members in that Michaelmas term in 1997, 670 names came forward as 'willing to nail their colours to the mast' and help with the work.

As the biggest Mission in terms of events, pS added a 'Digm Bar' to the evenings. In earlier Missions CICCU members followed the meetings up by taking their friends back to a college room or elsewhere for further conversation. The Digm Bar added a corporate setting for immediate follow-up. The nearby St Michael's Church gave permission for it to be set out as a café, with light refreshments served by graduates and other friends. Those attending the meetings were invited to go there, and in small groups at tables each night people raised questions and pursued discussion about the talks with Paul Weston, assistant missioners or CICCU members. (In fact, the title of 'assistant missioner' was dropped in favour of 'college guest' and later 'CU guest'.) Numbers coming to Mission meetings were lower in 1998 and this was one factor that kept discussion going about 'proclamation' evangelism.

In both these Missions the main appeal was for students to come to a subsequent four-week course. In 1995 this was 'Discovering Christianity' and in 1998 'The White Horse Tavern' – that title referring to the inn near St Catharine's College where in the sixteenth century the truths rediscovered by the Reformation were discussed. These courses involved cooperation with local churches.

The White Horse Tavern was run centrally for three nights per week over its four weeks. Those attending stayed in the same group throughout, sitting with its leaders over the meal and for the study/discussion, the leaders being Christians from the churches that offered venues and food. Speakers from Eden Chapel, St Andrew the Great and City Church provided the teaching from John's Gospel, based on a course written for the CICCU by Will Timmins, a UCCF staff member. In these ways CICCU was involved with churches, while avoiding denominational emphases and encouraging students to make up their own minds about which church to attend. Conversions came through these courses after both these Missions. 'Scores of Christians I now know can place the turning-point in their spiritual lives at the pS mission.'

PowerPoint presentation

One student from Sidney Sussex College was so enthused by the message of pS that he made a Microsoft PowerPoint presentation and ran it before the 350 at his Manufacturing Engineering lecture. He then got permission and showed the same presentation before first and second-year lectures throughout the Engineering Department – with hundreds of students being introduced to the gospel and the opportunity to explore Christianity at pS.

Another said, 'I learned that, in reaching my peers, there was no point in trying to be clever in witness. Nothing was to be gained by pandering to intellectualism or flattering inflated egos. My friends were simply sinners in need of a Saviour and needed the gospel, not clever ideologies.'

Rico Tice of All Souls, Langham Place, London, led the February 2001 Revelation Mission, back in the Guildhall. This took the 'Identity' presentation of Mark's Gospel and gave it a 'Revelation' cover to tie in with the Mission title. The meetings had a simple formula: live jazz greeted students as they arrived, and free cakes and soft drinks were served. Then, with the briefest introduction, came a gospel song and a testimony before Rico was on his feet. His talks, illustrated by relevant video clips and in other ways, were (in his repeated phrase) to let 'Jesus walk off the pages' of the Gospel and speak. Taking the main themes of Mark, he gave full weight to judgment and to grace, to forgiveness only through Christ's death in our place, and to the total cost of discipleship.

One member commented, 'I was thrilled that the emphasis on sin and judgment was unusually strong, yet Rico preached graciously with many tears. Revelation showed that even in our postmodern world, gospel proclamation through big missions could still be at the heart of the CICCU.'

Facing death

The testimony at the Friday evening meeting was by Laura Howarth, an Oxford graduate who was working in Cambridge as a UCCF CU worker. The evening's theme was on facing the future and Laura spoke on how she was facing death in her early thirties. Only three months earlier a consultant had diagnosed her as having inoperable lung cancer. She spoke with great honesty about how she had reacted to the news, affirming her quiet but firm trust in Jesus Christ to take her through death and into the glory of his presence for ever. One girl came to faith when Laura gave her testimony at the CICCU Bible Reading the week before and it left a deep impression on everyone. She died eleven months later on 23 January 2002.

About 700 attended the meetings each night and about 50 per cent were non-Christians. 'A great number of people made a stand for the gospel and held it out to their friends,' with many CICCU members aware that they did not want their friends to go to hell.

The follow-up to the Revelation Mission was based on the widely used *Christianity Explored* course developed by Rico Tice. A similar approach to follow-up operated again, the thinking being 'that CICCU should do what it can do and what churches cannot easily do – work inside colleges and coordinate the entire interdenominational mission – while a non-college-based course could perhaps be run by churches better than by CICCU'.

Proclamation still?

Through these years some pressure came to drop 'proclamation' as the main approach in evangelism. Some of this came in the mid-1980s, when John Wimber's 'Power Evangelism' was for a while an influence in some circles. Sometimes it arose when numbers at proclamation meetings were down or when a Mission attracted fewer than hoped. Some came from those who stressed relationship and friendship more than message. Some came because the confrontational nature of the gospel sat uneasily with current views of friendship and postmodern views of truth.

In 1999 a CICCU leader made this observation: 'There seemed to be two extremes running alongside each other. On the one hand were those who took a modernist approach, very cerebral and apologetic-based, often happier talking about issues than about Jesus. On the other, the postmoderns were busy seeking to "show people Jesus" or "share the person, not the ideology" (both phrases I heard bandied about). Living among non-Christians *was* evangelism, according to some, with the role of verbal communication downplayed. I think that this is just what the timid Christian wants to hear. This attitude just lets us off the hook, allowing us to feel better about living with people who are going to hell and yet saying nothing because "we don't want to lose their friendship". We tried to equip people for evangelism to deal with these two errors.'

It seemed to become harder to get Christians to invite non-Christians to talks and the CICCU encouraged members to know their friends well and to live out and share the gospel with them personally. Members knew that evangelism was hard work. At the same time many involved themselves thoroughly in all areas of college and university life such as sport, societies, college committees, Junior Common Rooms, the Union and faculties. The CICCU was far from being introverted. With students feeling themselves increasingly busy, the CICCU saw its responsibility to equip its members for appropriate witness in those spheres.

The CICCU held its course and did not lose its nerve, stressing both word proclamation and warm personal friendships. 'We reckoned that, if a non-Christian had the courage to come to a central event, then we should milk it and have a talk. Recently we have moved away from non-proclamation events such as film, drama, etc. and again encouraged evangelistic tea parties and college evangelistic events.'

Year-round evangelism

While the series of Missions took the headlines, successive CICCU Execs encouraged year-round evangelism. In several years college groups reported that evangelism was strong, that is, in distinction from central events. The centenary year, 1977, saw 'an increasing gap between most students and Christianity' and the CICCU tried various forms of regular evangelistic meetings.

The Sunday Evening or Sunday Night Addresses (SEAs or SNAs) were successors to the long-running Sunday Evening Sermons. Fewer usually attended these than the Saturday Bible Readings. Sometimes they tackled less conventional topics – 'What does Christianity have to say about sex?' – or a Christian professional pianist gave a recital and talked about his faith; both approaches were quite adventurous for 1981. Professor Donald MacKay attracted 600 to a meeting on science and faith in that year and 50 stayed behind to talk further. That, incidentally, was the year in which the CICCU book rep, Nick Land, set a record by reaching £10,000 in sales of IVP books to CICCU members.

In 1988 the SNA moved from Holy Trinity church, where it filled only the central part, to Selwyn College Diamond and prompted the speakers to be less formal and open to questions from the floor. The refreshments provided were an incentive to people to stay around afterwards. In later years the SNA moved from college to college to increase and spread ownership of it.

In 1990 the programme shifted to include a few more apologetics-based talks at lunchtime on Sundays, and these drew a different crowd. Nevertheless, 1993–4 had encouraging numbers at the SNAs. Postmodernism was hitting the scene – some exaggerated its importance, others underestimated it. One comment said that 'as far as I could work out, non-Christians were a weird mixture of modernist and postmodernist'. Hundreds came to the CICCU Carol Services in St Andrew the Great and sometimes 100-plus to the Sunday Night talks.

By 1998 the regular evangelistic events moved to Friday evenings, as being a freer time in a student's week. The thinking behind this was that in practice apologetics generally comes after people have started forming questions about Christianity. They therefore need, so the argument ran, to have at least some understanding of the gospel before they can react to it. CICCU did not want non-Christians to hear a message that was more apologetic or academic than biblical, so it decided that the Friday evenings should spend more time presenting the gospel than on formal apologetics, leaving members to take up their friends' questions or objections.

Free lunch

In 2001 Friday Lunchtime Talks started, with a free baguette lunch provided; these were a mixture of straight gospel talks and 'presenting the gospel through apologetics'. In the Michaelmas term 150–200 attended these. The Exec encouraged Christians to bring their friends, but to turn up anyway in order to learn how to answer people's questions. Weekly 'apologetics sheets' were available, giving guidelines on how to tackle issues. The FLTs were feeders into the *Christianity Explored* groups, which ran in almost every college and had over 100 non-Christians attending. Faculty Outreach Groups and many other evangelistic ventures also came more to the fore.

From the early 1980s Christians in Sport (CIS) ran regular dinners and other events for university and college-level sportspeople. The CIS judged them as successful or not by whether they reached and made the gospel clear to their specific target audiences. They were entirely complementary to the CICCU, most of those involved in CIS already being CICCU members. They concentrated solely on evangelism and left Bible study, follow-up and teaching to the CICCU.

Chapter 11
1977–2002
Pressures and questions

While the CICCU maintained its evangelistic calling, it faced many other challenges. Some arose within Christian circles; others concerned the CICCU's external relations with the university. This chapter looks at both spheres. In the former category came differences about Christian belief, witness and living.

Corporate prayer

One recurring theme was the place of prayer in general and of prayer meetings in particular. The long tradition of CICCU Daily Prayer Meetings (DPMs) changed in 1977–8, when Central Prayer Meetings (CPMs) came in, with different prayer topics for each day. 'We played down any idea that individuals should attend every day,' said one contemporary, but two years later the 'decline of the daily prayer meeting' was noted. In 1983 the Exec (the CICCU's Executive Committee) felt that attendance at the CPMs in the Henry Martyn Hall was poor because prayer was taking place in the college CICCU groups. They therefore reduced the number of CPMs to one on a Saturday.

In 1990 the CICCU group in St John's 'had a great crowd of students who started College DPMs; they were a great encouragement and drew around them a large number'. The next year, 1991, saw the CPM emphasized as the '*Colleges* PM, as a way of encouraging individual colleges to make more use of it'. At some stages, when attendances at the Bible Readings dropped as low as 120–150, the CPMs seemed to receive more emphasis than the Bible Readings (BRs) – a situation that the 1997 Exec redressed by underlining both the Bible and prayer.

By 2000 the central Colleges PM switched from lunchtime on Saturday to follow the early evening BR, with the aim of increasing the numbers at prayer. The move proved effective, as numbers at CPM jumped from 40 to 80 – and then in 2001 to 60–100. These timing changes, none hugely significant, signalled that the place of prayer was an ongoing concern, though many college groups had their own daily prayer meetings. One member felt strongly: 'Corporate prayer is vital, for God needs to raise the dead for people to be saved. Corporate Bible teaching is vital because, if we are going to serve God together by proclaiming Christ to our friends, we need God to teach us together – we need to be fed.'

Personal prayer

Personal daily Bible reading and prayer were matters harder to gauge, as the following mix of comments shows. In 1993 it was affirmed that 'we still keep encouraging people to have daily Quiet Times'. Four years later some thought 'that fewer CICCU members would have been spending time alone with God each day'. But in 1998 the churches and the CICCU 'actively encouraged personal prayer and Bible study; and I think that there is a high level of personal devotion. Most students are very busy, especially those involved in College sports; while they may not study the Bible first thing in the morning, they do endeavour to spend time in prayer and Bible study on most days.'

Practical Christian living

As CICCU members set out to live lives that commended Christ, many issues of lifestyle and behaviour surfaced. With nearly all colleges now mixed, questions of who was going out with whom were not uncommon. Dating and sexuality were always live issues, though at times some members were thought to be 'not clear on boy–girl relationships with non-Christians'. In the past some CICCU stalwarts had mildly frowned on romantic friendships and tradition had an unwritten rule that no president should fall in love with his vice-president, lest it impair the unity and focus of the Exec. No history of the CICCU, therefore, would be complete without one story like this from the 1970s: 'I broke the "greatest commandment" by falling in love with the Lady Vice-President. We are still happily married, with three committed Christian children (if you can't convert them, breed them!).' More seriously, the greater freedom between the sexes put much peer pressure on Christians. Facing the prevailing belief that having a good time is what matters, they needed fellowship and support to maintain a biblical stand.

By the 1990s student life was extremely pressurized – in contrast to the more leisured and leisurely lives that students seemed to enjoy in earlier decades. The question of the place of alcohol cropped up from time to time among Christians; while drunkenness and drug-taking were fairly common among students in general. Christians faced tough challenges to live godly lives in that context. No doubt some fell, but the witness of CICCU members' lifestyles supported their witness among their friends in sports teams and college societies as well as around lectures and labs.

Seminars or other occasional events tackled homo-sexuality and other topical issues. In 1993 Robin Weekes (Outreach Secretary on the Exec) opposed Richard Kirker of the Gay and Lesbian Christian Society and Peter Tatchell in a Union debate on 'This House believes that Gay is Good'. The motion was carried, though only by a surprisingly small majority.

The role of women

The place of women in the university, as in society gener-ally, changed markedly in the last quarter of the twentieth century, not least as college after college went mixed – leaving just three for women only. This had far-reaching effects, not only on the male–female student ratio.

In tracing this issue it is difficult to discern the extent to which views are affected by a changing society on the one hand or by Scripture on the other. Reflecting on the scene as mixed colleges were beginning to emerge in 1972, a CICCU leader wrote, 'We debated the desirability (or oth-erwise) of one male and one female College Representative working closely together. It seems strange now that we were so sensitive then.' By 1977 'we had the policy that a woman should do at least one public part of each week's BR meeting. How radical then, how archaic now!'

In 1983 the question came up for the first time of changing the constitution to allow a woman president, 'although we made no change. It took up a lot of time on Exec and in CICCU generally.' Two years later the consti-tution was changed so that the vice-president appointed would always be a woman. Then 1986 saw a vote on whether the president could be a woman: 'That was a hot issue, with strongly held views on both sides.' One woman member resigned her membership, convinced that the CICCU was about to invite female speakers – it did not. The vote at the General Committee, the body of Exec members and college representatives, failed to secure the necessary two-thirds majority for a woman president and the meeting agreed to put the issue on hold for three years. When the vote came up again in 1989, a clear mandate emerged for the constitution to be altered on that point.

With feelings occasionally running high among vocal minorities, the matter was handled overall in a good spirit, with the desire to keep as many members as possible united for the CICCU's main task. Differences remained (and remain) on this question, but then so did they on another issue of that time – whether Christians should do academic work on Sundays.

A woman president

In 1993–4 came the first and so far the only woman president, Ursula Mayr-Harting (now Weekes). One of the most obvious candidates had been ill for most of the preceding year and was not physically up to the demands of the post. When she was invited to consider it, the main query in her mind was 'Is the presidency of the CICCU a headship role?' If it were, she felt that she could not take it, given her convictions about the Bible's teaching on women. She and others concluded that 'it was not a headship role akin to that of pastor-teachers' and that it would 'not involve direct teaching authority over my contemporaries or any ultimate pastoral oversight of students, since CICCU is not a church'. She still thinks that 'it is unhelpful to see the presidency as a headship role, whether man or woman, not least because of the pressure it unnecessarily places on the person'; but believes that 'it is more helpful for the CICCU for the Presidents to be male, because they model Christian leadership to fellow students'.

'From the female perspective, if I ask "What would have been the best way to encourage my male Christian contemporaries to grow into mature Christian leaders while at

Cambridge?", then I think the answer probably does not lie in my having become President of CICCU. As President I felt that I must try to model being a godly woman, not a woman trying to be a man. In the event I worked extremely closely with the Vice-President (Nathan Buttery) and in a sense he was as much President as I was.'

National publicity

One of the unforeseen side-effects of Ursula's appointment was some national interest. The vote to appoint her as president took place in November 1992 and coincided with the vote in the General Synod of the Church of England on the ordination of women (to which, incidentally, she was opposed). Some evangelical church leaders became needlessly concerned that the CICCU was losing its way doctrinally and it was more these external pressures that made her initiation somewhat stressful. 'CICCU itself was remarkably undisturbed by the whole thing and we just got on with the task of evangelising students.' The constitutional position in 2002 was that a male or a female could be elected as either president or vice-president, though the general assumption seemed to be that the president would be male.

In 1994–5 the question of women speakers came up, but 'at that time we felt that it would divide too much, so we avoided it – and were too busy with a main mission'. The following year's Exec decided against it by six to two.

Relationships with Cambridge churches

Once the two main churches for CICCU members had been the Round Church (which later moved into and became known as St Andrew the Great) and Eden Chapel, with Holy Trinity joining them as time went on. Over this period other churches became attractive to students, including Anglican, Baptist, Brethren, Presbyterian and several new or charismatic churches. This mix was reflected, though not always proportionately, in CICCU membership.

Churches differed in their concept of student work. Some explicitly sought to build students up on Sundays through Bible teaching in order to send them back equipped to witness in their colleges and faculties for the rest of the week. On this basis some encouraged students to go to CICCU college and central meetings rather than attend to their church midweek activities. Some schemes of student associate membership and of hospitality with church families aimed to support this vision. Those churches tended to have a higher proportion of their students in the CICCU. Others expressed their vision for students by drawing them more into their own discipleship, cell or other midweek structures, somewhat apart from university life.

This difference in part reflected the charismatic or noncharismatic stance of the churches, though CICCU members generally were willing to live with the differences, provided that they could all get on together with witness in the colleges. Differences over what most members regarded as 'church distinctives' were not new. Tension over similar matters had emerged before and first surfaced in these years when 'Reformed' or strongly conservative emphases became more prominent. In the 1970s one observer noted that there was both a 'heavy Reformed coterie and also interesting charismatic challenges'. In the 1980s, for example, a few debated over Isaiah 53 and what it taught about the extent of the atonement.

Reformed emphases

The CICCU handled these issues, sometimes with difficulty, but generally better than the wider evangelical world, which was often troubled and very divided. 'In the 1980s some "charismatics" wanted more lively singing for longer, while some "Reformed" were strongly opposed to those modern songs. We kept together by focusing on our aims . . .' The question of musical preferences came up quite often; generally it was simply a sign or symptom of people's differences, rather than being of their essence. Both the Reformed and the charismatics suffered unfairly, at opposite poles, from pejorative adjectives such as 'hard-line' or 'woolly'.

From time to time some of more Reformed persuasion caused some fear for the CICCU's unity. Because the CICCU did not adopt their stance, some set up the 'Cambridge University Evangelical Fellowship' for a time alongside or, as some thought, in competition with the CICCU. However, a change of heart led to the closing of this as a separate society. Those of Reformed persuasion kept their convictions, stayed in the CICCU and put their hearts into expressing the unity in the gospel that had been restored.

A kind of mirror image of that debate arose later, centred on 'Fusion'. This was a national movement developed in the 1990s largely by some of the new or charismatic church groupings. In Cambridge, for example, two of the main charismatic churches supported Fusion, but another's policy was not to back it. Fusion's methodological distinctive was its insistence on the cell structure as the way of working.[76] It believed in a 'unity in diversity' that encouraged each group or church to express its own distinctives. This was different from the CICCU's 'unity in the gospel' convictions, which urged people to put inter-church differences aside for the sake of the lost.

In the Lent term 1997 these issues particularly affected the CICCU group in Trinity College. Those involved in what ended so sadly had been good and close friends. Some had led others of them to Christ. It was never personal animosities that prompted or stirred the differences.

Christian love had been a reality for them, even though much pain ensued when issues arose that all believed to be more important than personal ties.

A new group needed?

Some began to feel that the college needed a new kind of group, with a different emphasis – to focus more on discipleship than did the CICCU with its prime aim of evangelism. The CICCU college representatives felt that discipleship was more properly the role of the churches. They also believed that, in a college with only a few Christians, a second evangelical group would needlessly divide witness just where it most needed to be united.

In Michaelmas 1997 some Christians were led to leave the Trinity CICCU group and form a Fusion group. Personal bonds remained, but the separation had its effect; the CICCU group was not large in any case and the division left it with few active members – in the term leading up to the pS mission. They felt that a sectional emphasis had been elevated to where it divided the gospel witness and excluded some Christians. They could not endorse that, even though that put personal relationships under strain. They also noted that on some of the issues the charismatic churches were not agreed, so that the division was never on charismatic/non-charismatic lines. They further felt that the biblical message was being compromised by insistence on some 'gospel-plus' elements.

The sad episode did little to commend evangelical witness in the college, either to its undergraduate or, when it came to their notice, to its senior members. In the event the CICCU group grew through the Mission and its follow-up: a number of first-years came to Christ and key students discovered for themselves the meaning of the gospel and the value of Bible teaching.

All concerned in this and subsequent local difficulties

acknowledged an evangelical doctrinal basis, but differed over what principles guided them in practice. Among the questions that arose were the following. Should the prime focus of a (CU) group be discipleship or evangelism? Should guidance be claimed through direct 'words from God'? What place should Bible study have in the life of an individual, group or cell? How did cell differ from a Bible study group? What of experiences or phenomena such as tongues, physical signs and manifestations? Can a higher level of Christian experience be reached? What of claims that revival would come to the college? Is 'belonging before believing' biblical evangelism? And should church or denominational distinctives have any place – the defining place – in a non-denominational CU group?

Substance or style?

Some wondered if such differences were more of style than of substance – over, for example, whether there should be more or less singing or 'worship' in meetings. In that case, agreeing to differ could have been a way forward. But to many this was much more than a 'style' issue; it was about truth content, not merely presentation. At stake were questions about which truths were central to biblical evangelism and vital for the unbeliever to hear.

Crucial differences seemed to be on the priority of making the gospel known, the duty to express unity in witness and the governing place of the Bible. Some differences of approach were over where the main emphasis was put; or over what was not said or not included as well as over what was said. The omissions were as significant as the affirmations. Whatever the disputes on the issues that arose, if the focus was on them, it was not on what chiefly mattered. The CICCU believed that the content of the gospel could not be assumed, but needed always to be explicit – for example, God's wrath and judgment, not just his mercy and love; humanity's guilt and lostness, not just its lack of fulfilment or purpose; hell as well as heaven; the substitutionary sacrifice of Christ as imperative for forgiveness; the wonder of undeserved grace; the call to repentance and the serious cost of following Christ.

Before the firing squad

Helen Roseveare had been converted in Cambridge during the Second World War and had given her life to missionary service in the Congo. As one of the CICCU's honorary vice-presidents, she was involved in discussing some of the issues that arose in and around the Trinity CICCU group. She posed this question: 'What is going to stand you in good stead when you are a missionary, as I trust you all will be? I tell you that three times I had to stand before a firing squad and thought that I was going to be shot (in the Simba rebellion in the Congo). What helped me then was the actual words of Scripture that I had learned when I was in the CICCU.'

Successive CICCU generations wrestled with these issues, trying – as Helen Roseveare – to hold on to what was ultimately important. In the late 1970s one CICCU leader took this approach: 'I was shocked on arrival to discover that 90 per cent of CICCU were Anglicans and thus mistaken on infant baptism! As a non-Anglican I was in a strong position to argue with my pro-charismatic friends. I put it to them that I was prepared for the sake of unity in the gospel *not* to seek to persuade fellow CICCU members of believer's baptism since, by virtue of evangelicals disagreeing, it was by definition a secondary issue – even though I knew I was right and 90 per cent of CICCU wrong! So please would they – for the sake of unity in the gospel – desist from charismatic pressurising on a secondary issue.'

Some twenty years later a changing evangelical world

prompted this comment: 'The increase of students from charismatic backgrounds meant that we kept needing to clarify the difference between the content of what we were doing and saying (which we did not want to change – the historic doctrines) and the style in which we did things (on which we were happy to be flexible). Allowing for the breadth of church background within CICCU was possible, but up to a point . . .'

The threat of liberalism had been relatively easy to deal with, or at least to recognize, compared to these questions. Another wrote, 'If the CICCU is to last as an interdenominational student group, that unity must be based on the gospel. That is, the CICCU has a gospel priority first and is interdenominational second. CICCU is only interdenominational on the basis of the primary place of the gospel . . . On the issues over which we disagree, we must be gracious and hold to primary beliefs – and agree that secondary things are indeed secondary.'

Crisp focus statement

In this period the CICCU sharpened its focus into this crisp statement: 'The CICCU exists to make Jesus Christ known to students in Cambridge.' This was to keep the vision clear within CICCU, but also to show that CICCU did not try to embrace all Christian obligations and did not want to trespass on the churches' proper spheres.

The CICCU held regular and thorough discussions with a range of church leaders in order to keep in touch and clarify issues. Many good relationships were formed and channels of communication kept open. The CICCU's policy was not to comment on issues that fell within the remit of the churches, but to encourage members to search the Scriptures and come to their own conclusions. The help of several churches was particularly useful in the follow-up to missions. And the CICCU leadership, while chosen primarily to find the most suitable people for the posts, also sought to have members from different church backgrounds who were united in the gospel.

Among the matters discussed were relationships with Fusion groups in several colleges. Their place and role were not always clear to everyone affected and were a potential cause of misunderstanding. Were they simply the student cells or ministry of one or two churches – in effect, denominational groups? If so, should they draw in people from other churches and what if other churches wanted to start groups? Or were they, through such activities as welcoming members from other churches and having a stall at the Freshers' Fair, *de facto* another interdenominational society? Either way, did they complement or strengthen a united non-denominational witness? These issues remained matters for ongoing discussion and concern.

Through these situations the CICCU tried to do three things: to keep its specific gospel aims clear; on that basis to welcome diversity of church background in its membership and activities; and to maintain a unity in Christ in the core biblical truths for the sake of non-Christians. Despite some differences, the work of the gospel went on.

Always the guiding principle was the firm belief that the three or four years of an undergraduate's life are an unrepeatable opportunity for the gospel. Out of love to God and others, that opportunity must be taken; and it can be best taken only by peers, that is, by fellow students who are members in the colleges and united in that gospel. That called for a single-mindedness and a degree of sacrifice if others are to hear, for nothing was more important for eternity.

On the university scene

What of external relations? CICCU's standing in the university at large was good for most of this period, but around the time of Missions it occasionally went through bouts of criticism or opposition. This was nothing new; indeed, the criticisms were generally less fierce than in the 1940s and 1950s.

In the 1970s the CICCU met greater, if slightly grudging, politeness. This was probably because it was the largest student religious body. It had over 400 actual members and more at its biggest meeting, the weekly Bible Reading. In total, around 1,000 were in Bible Study groups in colleges – nearly 10 per cent of all undergraduates.

There was no serious sizeable alternative to the CICCU, as there had been when theologically liberal groups were dominant. This fact continued to surprise some senior churchmen and others who had backed the latter groups. One commented that the SCM groups had been expected to sweep the field in the expansion of higher education during the 1960s. That eminent commentator later reflected that 'we lost and you (UCCF) won'. He was referring to the general growth of the Christian Unions of the UCCF and, while disagreeing with UCCF's basis, acknowledged that its growth was due to the fact that CICCU and the other CUs stuck closely 'to Jesus, the Bible and prayer'. That was an analysis that the CICCU would want always to be true.

In that situation the CICCU sometimes had a larger fringe than before. That meant that its members were no longer compelled to think about the difference between evangelical and liberal views or to decide which to adopt. That difference had always been a spur, though sometimes painful, for CICCU members to sort out what beliefs were or were not worth fighting for. A larger fringe obscured for some the need to defend and stand for truth; on the other hand, many who began on the fringe ended up with clearer convictions as they made friends, discussed and engaged with the Bible.

Raising the old charges

Secular voices in the university ignored or tolerated the CICCU most of the time, but were always alert to raise the old charges. *Varsity* newspaper, for example, carried less than complimentary articles during the 1989 John Chapman Mission (maybe they thought an Aussie a fair target), but with no outright hostility. 'At other times we were slammed in *Varsity* for being over-zealous. I think that we were likened to the Ku-Klux-Klan on one occasion.' The 1998 mission had an enormous but unfriendly profile in the university: 'Three weeks of letters in *Varsity*, alternative poster campaigns, anti-CICCU fliers stapled round cycle handlebars outside colleges, the 25-foot banner hanging from the University Church and advertising the mission turned upside down, interviews on the university radio show and an article in the national press (yes, *The Guardian*).'

The Transmission mini-Mission that Vaughan Roberts led in February 2000 came under strident fire, with letters and leaders carrying all the hoary accusations of fundamentalism, intolerance, etc. To the well-rehearsed objections to the CICCU's beliefs were added similar reactions to the CICCU's stance on ethical issues, particularly in relation to sexuality and to homosexual practice. But, as sometimes happens, a non-Christian appeared in defence of the press-battered CICCU. One letter to *The Cambridge Student* was forthright: 'I find myself in the unusual position of defending CICCU in light of the criticism their "Transmission" campaign has received. I am in no way a Christian and I disagree with Christianity on most fronts, but I am a passionate believer in free speech.

'Transmission may seem ubiquitous, yet that does not mean that people are unable to make up their own minds. It is my feeling that CICCU is being criticized not because of their methods, but because of their content. I have found personally that the repeal of Section 28, rent strikes and even the march for the Cambridge two have been more "in your face" than Transmission. Interestingly, they are accompanied with the assumption, so often levelled against evangelical Christians, that those who campaign for these issues have the moral high ground. They assume that they are right and, if I disagree, I am wrong, not just intellectually but morally as well. Why is CICCU convicted of ramming their moral code down people's throats when those who campaign vigorously for the repeal of Section 28 and advocating rent strikes are applauded for their actions? Why should someone be criticized for being "conservative"? Is it simply because the repeal of Section 28 is right whereas Christian conservatism is wrong? However, it seems as though, just because CICCU are preaching something that is not "mainstream", they are being asked to refrain. It seems that, despite the progress we have made in democracy in the last one hundred years, some points of view are "allowed" and some are not.

'Fortunately for myself, I appear to be on the "acceptable" side for now, but I do not want to live in a society where I cannot disagree with the popular opinion . . .' (name and college supplied).

Not only that, but Transmission received a review in *Varsity* the following week that was as favourable as it was heavy with irony. Transmission produced no CD, but the reviewer used world-of-music terms to make some clever points: 'In the beginning was the *Paradigm Shift* album, and you'll remember how that shook up the local scene. Now they're back from the wilderness with this new offering, *Transmission* . . . I've listened to these tunes religiously and so should you. Move over Faith No More. This is CICCU.'

On the whole *Varsity* and *The Cambridge Student* were

much quieter about the 2001 Mission. Maybe that was a decision not to give the CICCU so much even negative publicity. Or maybe it was growing student apathy?

Distribution forbidden

In 1995 and 1998 all the colleges allowed CICCU members to give out Gospels, either door to door or at least via college pigeon holes. In 2001 some college authorities contacted their CICCU groups part-way through the project and forbade them to distribute Gospels to their fellow college members and friends. That seemed a curb on religious liberty – as one called it, 'an outrageous infringement of student rights'.

A related issue surfaced in May 1998. The university authorities rejected the constitution of the Christian Music and Drama Society (Ark) because it did not contain this regulation clause: 'The membership of the society shall be open to all members of the university, regardless of race, gender, religion, sexual orientation or political opinion.' Ark had the same declaration of membership as the CICCU: 'I desire to declare my faith in Jesus Christ as my Saviour, my Lord and my God.'

Status lost

Later the CICCU found itself in the same position. The authorities deemed its constitution unacceptable and just before Easter 2000 withdrew its long-held status as a university society. This arose because the CICCU had amended its constitution on a small matter and had to resubmit it to the university junior proctor. When the authorities read it, they said that the CICCU's membership declaration was discriminatory on religious grounds, since it involved a belief statement. The loss of status did not seem too heavy a practical blow in itself. It would mean loss of insurance cover, which could be replaced at a cost, but it would not affect such matters as the CICCU's standing with the Cambridge University Student Union or prevent the CICCU having its stand at the Freshers' Fair.

However, some read the judgment as flawed in principle and potentially dangerous as a precedent. Consultation with Senior Friends, church leaders (particularly at St Andrew the Great) and UCCF reinforced this concern. They pointed out that this rejection might affect the CICCU's freedom of witness in the future and that the outcome of this case could also have good or bad repercussions for Christian Unions elsewhere. Senior Friends and university academics accompanied the CICCU to the authorities. They went armed with a report from 'The Voice of the Universities' (then known as 'The Committee of Vice-Chancellors and Principals'). This prestigious secular body set out unambiguous statements in defence of societies with a closed or definite membership.

That excellent report declared, for example, that 'no group shall be denied the right to organize themselves within the Union on the grounds of their views, beliefs, policies or objectives. No existing club shall be disestablished or subject to particular restrictions on account of its members' views, beliefs, policies or objectives. It shall be permissible for particular clubs or societies to impose restrictions on eligibility to join or participate on such grounds as national origins, ethnicity, religion, gender or sexual orientation.' The title of that report was *Extremism and Intolerance on Campus* and further sample quotations and publication details are given in the notes.[77] When the authorities weighed the arguments and that supporting evidence, they reinstated the CICCU as a university society later in the Easter Term 2000.

Chapter 12
1977–2002
From Cambridge to the world

'Of the eight of us on the Exec in the 1980s, six were men and two women. Three men are now overseas missionaries, one is in the ministry here and two are serving Christ in industry. Of the two women, one is married to a minister, the other to a university lecturer. All eight are strongly committed to the faith, to their local churches and to their families. All eight marriages are strong … Quite an encouraging statistic.

'By the time I left Cambridge the call to missions to Muslims had got under my skin (as much as anything, through taking part in the Islamic Nations prayer group) and so it remained. I worked for three and a half years in a factory in Rochdale, where most of my fellow-workers were Pakistani, and I began to learn Urdu. I then married, trained and went to Pakistan, where we have been ever since. The Bible teaching I received at CICCU, the sense of teamwork on the Exec … have had a profound effect on my subsequent development and work.'

That was Tim Green, president in 1981–2, giving a personal example of the CICCU's influence beyond

Cambridge. This has always been a major part of its story: Christians living for and living out the gospel in Cambridge, then moving out into wider society and into the world beyond.

Social concerns

Many CICCU members were concerned for social justice issues and involved in them. The existence in Cambridge of the Jubilee Centre helped many by bringing clear information, challenging thought and prompting involvement in the UK and for the wider world. The CICCU itself had no 'social justice' group and no equivalent programme. This was not because it was unconcerned about the major issues or insensitive to the way they affected millions. It was simply because the CICCU did not believe that it should try to embrace all the duties that were proper for a Christian. Believers were responsible to work out what they should think and do about many issues in church and society – everything from baptism to Third World debt. The CICCU, however, existed 'to make Jesus Christ known to students in Cambridge' and to do what directly supported that focus. It was there for that mission and its particular and limited aims meant that it stuck to those, while urging members to pursue their wider obligations through their churches, the Jubilee Centre or in other ways.

Thinking Christianly

At various points in this period CICCU leaders and members tried to give more importance to finding help to think Christianly about academic topics and their relation to Christian truth. The CICCU often, though not always consistently, also sensed that it should be doing more to help CU members to think biblically about their future life and service in work and in society. Stimulus was given to consider missionary work or home ministry, but not often about other callings or to think about a theology of work. Members increasingly needed a biblical framework to guide them in thinking about aims and ambitions in a world that prized success, salary, self-fulfilment and satisfaction.

Occasional seminars or conferences on vocation or similar themes had tried to address these needs – but occasionally, rather than regularly. One of these in the 1970s aimed 'to make clear that in the range of careers open there was opportunity for mission. In addition to a general talk on "Vocation: living in the world", there were Saturday seminars on Management, Civil Service, Architecture, Engineering, Finance, Medicine, Social Work, Education, Research, Medicine, Law... on being a professional Christian abroad, on being a missionary and on being a housewife. On the Sunday, seminars tackled involvement in the local church . . . and in the local community; and Christian lifestyle.' Seldom has such a comprehensive programme been put on with a view to postgraduate Christian living. It changed a lot of people's minds.

Some members regret that 'we failed to address the wider issues concerning our place in the University. We were clearly benefiting from a superb education, but what was our responsibility to those denied such an education? To what extent was the university exacerbating social division rather than breaking it down? Was Christianity elitist and, if so, what was the Christian's response to this?'

International students

The CICCU did, however, try to give attention to the wider world within its walls – that of international students. Of 15,500 full-time students in the university in 2001, 11,000 were undergraduates and 4,500 postgraduates. Of the latter, 15 per cent (nearly 700) were internationals, from around 100 countries. Some undergraduates, of course, were also from other countries. When faced with this challenge, most CICCU years had a sense of their failure to take adequate initiatives to reach and befriend international students.

The CICCU has sometimes had energetic and visionary 'International Secretaries'. 'There is a growing international student population in Cambridge that is poorly reached by undergraduates' was a typical comment. And it was obviously true that an eighteen-year-old undergraduate, still a new Christian, would not be best placed to help and discuss with a PhD student from, say, India or China who might be nearly twice his or her age. 'However,' it continued, 'the Cambridge Christian Graduate Society met every foreign student at either the bus or train station, offered assistance on arrival and ran small Bible study groups through the year, mainly for graduates.' The CGS greatly enhanced students' efforts and in 2000 the CICCU renewed its efforts through a weekly venture that welcomed international students into homes for a meal and an optional Bible study.

The title 'International Secretary' took over as a post on the CICCU Exec from 'Missionary Secretary' around 1975 – and not without some disquiet. The arguments in favour of the change included the belief that in some minds 'missionary' conjured up a colonial and paternalistic past. Others felt that the change might indicate or initiate a reduced sense of sacrifice and obligation to Christ's Great Commission to the ends of the earth. The CICCU's long missionary tradition seemed sometimes to be a burden too heavy for some young undergraduates. The Cambridge Seven were writ large in the annals of the CICCU, as were the later 'Cambridge Seventy' – students who pledged themselves to serve Christ overseas.

Ebb and flow of interest

Interest in world mission ebbed and flowed. The 1970s had a background sense of 'echoes of a glorious past', but this was sometimes more a weight than a stimulus. 'We well understood our heritage, though the days of the 70 had gone.' Nevertheless, 'we held missionary breakfasts regularly. A significant number from my year ended up working overseas, either as missionaries or in other employment.' At other points 'world and missionary vision were strong, with flourishing prayer groups. The SE Asia group in 1977 was effectively for the work of the Overseas Missionary Fellowship; 15–20 regulars met in Hugh Balfour's magnificent room in Sidney Sussex, where he was Boat Club captain. We had a memorable visit from Helen Roseveare, who spoke to a jam-packed crowd in Holy Trinity.' Another comment made no reference to missionary calling, but of a good flow into the ordained ministry and into other full-time Christian work.

In the 1980s missionary concern was reasonably strong. 'Numbers at world prayer groups were never as high as we would have liked, but quite a few functioned and there were missionary reps. in all the colleges. There was quite a movement to send 80 missionaries in that decade, but I don't know how many went overseas in the end.' High priority was given to world vision, though some did not see this as 'core' activity. 'World vision continued to be inspiring, though it was always something of a minority concern. It was still very difficult to engage fully with the fact that we belonged to a world that existed outside Cambridge, let alone outside the UK. One memorable quote came from George Verwer of Operation Mobilisation at a missionary breakfast; he said that he could not believe that people with such intelligence could be such geographical ignoramuses.'

In the 1990s 'world and missionary vision was quite high and we had an excellent International Secretary. However, not many of our contemporaries were thinking of overseas work, while many were thinking of full-time paid Christian work in this country.' 'We tried to expand world prayer groups – and had huge sales of the latest *Operation World*.'[78] 'As ever, the faithful few were very interested; the rest (to our shame) were not. This missionary aim of the CICCU seemed at times to be tacked on and was not the focus of many. Only eight per cent of CICCU membership went into full-time ministry, and those mostly in the UK.'

Often there seemed to be little prayer and enthusiasm for overseas mission – perhaps a reflection of the church at large. On the other hand, links developed and grew strong between UCCF's central region, of which CICCU was a part, and the IFES movement in Belarus. Students visited each other's universities and CU groups each year to great mutual benefit. And out of the eight members on one Exec, seven had already been on short-term overseas missions or were thinking about this for the future; they felt it important to stress the third (world vision) aim of the CICCU.

The CICCU held regular International Breakfasts to spread information and a sizeable 'Romans 10:14 Group' (formerly the ''90s Group') was considering missionary work. In the face of sometimes confrontational and assertive Islamic witness a 'Cross and Crescent' course was the major focus in an Islamic Awareness Week; over thirty students learnt about Islam and about engaging with Muslims through friendship and discussion.

College groups and world mission

One small change had some effect on world mission concern. It was the transition from 'College CICCU groups' to the more self-conscious title of 'College CUs'. This aimed to strengthen witness in colleges and stimulate good initiatives in evangelism, rather than leaving it all to the CICCU centrally. It achieved some of those goals in some of the colleges. However, it almost certainly weakened the sense of belonging to the CICCU as a whole and so had a bearing on world vision. It was difficult for a small college CU to give anything like a broad introduction to global mission, partly because it could never get a comparable range of suitable speakers. And any small group is more susceptible to the preferences, limitations or blind spots of its current leader. The change may unintentionally have reduced world awareness and the sense of missionary challenge.

Successive CICCU members tried to address these matters and keep a world vision alive. In 2001 the title of 'world prayer groups' changed to 'world evangelism prayer groups', to make the focus clearer. And after the 1998 mission had underlined the CICCU's unity, several 'College CUs' reverted to being 'College CICCU groups' in order to identify with the CICCU centrally.

A Second Missionary Day

Back in 1931 many Cambridge men attended the Twelfth Inter-Varsity Conference of the Inter-Varsity Fellowship of Evangelical Unions – the IVF (which became the UCCF). Its magazine reported that 'very many met Jesus face to face. That meant the "I" crossed out and a new willingness to be obedient to him, at whatever cost. The conference had an extra day as a Second Missionary Day. The missionary speakers turned our thoughts again and again to the fields "white unto harvest". The appalling need of the peoples of the world was brought vividly before us. The realization of the need of those in darkness deepened. The Call came with even greater insistence and many of us were facing "the Problem of a Life Work".'

Such emphases and such an atmosphere seemed unfamiliar to the later CICCU. Among those considering gospel ministry the focus shifted almost imperceptibly from overseas to this country. However, that shift could in time yield candidates for overseas as well. At the same time, and sadly, the CICCU made a smaller long-term contribution to IFES ministries than it had previously done, though several went on IFES and other short-term summer teams every year and some on IFES year teams.

However, comparisons are difficult and unfair, since many factors beyond the CICCU's control have changed, in the world and in the church. In society at large jobs and careers reversed away from the old idea of serving one company for life; changes and projects and time out became the pattern. In missions the trend grew for candidates to be accepted for limited periods, with the sense of calling to a 'life work' welcome but not a requirement. If this had a down side, it also had some plus points and numbers of former CICCU members gave periods to serving overseas. In addition, many followed professional callings or careers abroad, some in countries closed to the gospel.

The missionary call is still heard in Cambridge: 'The Christian global perspective that CICCU presented managed to get through all the defences I put up (only in my last term did I attend my one and only missionary breakfast), so that I am now a cross-cultural Christian worker in the Arab world.'

That same individual continued, 'It is probably harder to be an evangelical Christian at university these days than it was 20 years ago. Harder, certainly, to stand for any moral absolutes. To do so is to risk victimisation by the politically correct. Yet, having lived many years in the Islamic world, western culture in general seems to be cast adrift in a sea of relativism, with no anchor points and no star to steer by. When tolerance is our only cultural absolute, where will we end up? The West holds all the trump cards politically, economically and militarily, but has lost its way spiritually and is living on borrowed time. The point of all this is that today's evangelical students have to stand firm in their theological and moral convictions, even if that brings unpopularity. Their time will come if they "hang in there" now – just as CICCU's founding fathers had to in the days of SCM supremacy.'

A later CICCU member reflected along similar lines, 'I don't know how we as evangelicals would adapt to being a minority in a multi-cultural, multi-faith society and have humility, gentleness and respect for those around us, while at the same time retaining our confidence in the truth of the gospel and the lordship of Christ.'

Going on after graduation

Records of CICCU membership have never been preserved consistently enough to allow a full analysis of what happened to them after they graduated. The parable of the sower obviously applies in every era and the sad cases of the New Testament, such as Demas, 'in love with this present world' (2 Timothy 4:10), still have parallels. Yet whenever the periodic rumours of fall-away rates circulate, no-one ever backs them up with facts or figures or, indeed, applies the same yardstick to churches.

By contrast, the evidence shows a great many going on with God. Several Cambridge Prayer Fellowship groups have kept going to keep ex-members in touch and these always give news of many still running hard in the race. Indeed, the CPF of as far back as 1930 was still running at the time of writing, even though the majority of its original members had graduated to the heavenly university. That of 1973 still had over three dozen members, several in the ministry and others serving in Bangladesh, Central

Asia, Ethiopia, Israel, Kenya, Malaysia, Portugal and Spain. Of the Exec of 1955, the year of Billy Graham's first CICCU Mission, some spent their lives in overseas mission (with Wycliffe Bible Translators or the Red Sea Mission Team), some in ministry in the UK, others as Christians in teaching, editing or other callings.

A graduate from the 1970s, now a GP and a trainer of GPs, echoed that experience: 'A bit worrying, isn't it, the incredible level of stability and maturity the entire Exec are displaying 25 years on. All doing responsible jobs, all still committed to the church, still married to our original partners.' People kept going on with God in a variety of callings, for instance: 'By the end of my year I was convinced that my role in life was to be out there for Christ, involved in the world rather than focused in service in a specifically Christian context . . . I was elected a local councillor and then stood in a Westminster election.'

Finding where they went

One of the few systematic attempts to investigate CICCU members came in the 1970s when one Exec processed the results of a questionnaire of CICCU members who had left two, five and ten years earlier. The overwhelming evidence led them to this conclusion: 'If you are committed in the CU, you will be committed to Christ and his church when you leave.' Their consequent exhortation was 'So keep on keeping on. Fan into flame the gift of God within you through the gospel!'

An Exec from the 1990s echoed what many college CICCU year groups have found – that they had made links for the long term, not just for one year: 'We became the best of friends and continue to meet to pray for and support each other. I remember thinking that God had not put us together merely for that year, but for the friendship and fellowship beyond. That still provides mutual encouragement and a level of accountability. Because we came from a range of backgrounds (currently one from Vineyard, one Baptist, one charismatic Anglican and three conservative evangelical Anglicans) there is something extremely positive about our continued unity and the challenge to each other to think.' Another's responsibilities in the CICCU 'began to open my eyes to the lesson of God equipping us for what he calls us to do, and so to rise, trusting him, to the challenge. CICCU as a whole gave me a love for the Bible and for teaching that fires mind and heart.'

CICCU and ministry

Many testify to the connection between what they learned through the CICCU and the fact that they subsequently went into Christian ministry. Four examples represent the experience of many others. One was sure that 'I would not be ordained if I had not had the opportunities that CICCU gave me.' A second said, 'CICCU helped me to see the importance and value of ministry. That was the first taste of Christian leadership that I had ever had and I'm sure that one of the reasons why I am now in full-time paid Christian work is because of being given those responsibilities. Much of what I learned there I am using in my work now.' A third acknowledged that 'it was one of the shaping factors in directing me into full-time Christian ministry later on, after several years in scientific research'. A fourth said simply that 'the early experience of responsibility equipped me for what I am doing now in gospel ministry. My UCCF staff worker told me when I began as President that I would have more spiritual responsibility in that year than I would have for years. He was right! It was too much, too young . . . but it was invaluable training in spiritual leadership.'

Accepting responsibility

The CICCU gave responsibility to a large number of people every year in many different ways. The Exec's duties were the most obvious, but equally important were college representatives, to whom it fell to arrange the evangelism, Bible study and prayer in their college, to relate to chaplains and authorities and to handle the administration behind all that. They had responsibility for the CICCU members plus the many more who attended college Bible studies and other activities. Many other members were involved in world mission groups, international student outreach, publicity, Mission planning and countless other tasks. The CICCU centrally was much larger than the average church – and some college groups were sizeable too. In addition to the more obviously 'spiritual' duties the CICCU also gave many people more than an introduction to person-management, time-organization, handling stress, public speaking, dealing with conflict, and much more.

In such ways the CICCU obviously had a considerable influence on many members, though sometimes the effect of carrying large responsibilities had a down side. 'We grew enormously doing the work and for that we are hugely grateful to God. However, the demands of the responsibilities took us off the coal face and as a result our personal evangelism suffered.' For one it had in part 'a negative effect as cynicism and prejudice were great battles. I felt a huge temptation to take up a condescending attitude with many people. At times I felt quite dried out as a Christian.' For another it also had 'a huge effect. It probably made me proud, which I needed to unlearn, but I hope it also made me trust God more, lead others better, study the Bible more hungrily and look for help sooner.'

For one person it meant that 'I lost a grade in finals and gained far more in terms of leadership training! To be allowed leadership responsibility at such an age made for very rapid growth. I remember meeting a staff worker from another large student movement who was spending a year in Cambridge. He asked what I saw as the secret of leadership training in the CICCU. I asked him how many full-time staff workers they had at his university back home. The answer was five or six. I asked him who led the activities and made the decisions in the campus work there. He said it was mainly the Staff. "There's your answer", I said.'

For many the experience of fellowship in the CICCU was eye-opening. 'Having had a somewhat sheltered denominational background, exposure to other Christians (Anglican, Presbyterian, charismatic, etc.) with a heart for the Bible and for their friends to be saved was enlightening. The temptation for pride and self-sufficiency was always present, but being given responsibility was an incredible privilege. It was great to work with an amazingly gifted and diverse group of Christians.' Another who 'came from a small, obscure church background' found that the effect of the duties that fell to him was 'immense, leading to a time of great growth in understanding the Scriptures'.

Learning lessons: discernment

All these experiences taught many lessons. One leader wanted to emphasize to his successors the need for discernment. To leaders he said, 'You will be faced with different people with sincerely held beliefs, urging you to go in significantly different directions. Some will be potty. The key gift you will need will be discernment, and, in exercising it, you will have to be very careful not to become cynical.' And to members, 'Enjoy the special opportunities of Cambridge to explore your faith, including at an intellectual level, and to share it with others.' Another wanted to say to later members that the 'CICCU's stand for a biblical evangelicalism was increasingly important as the heritage of the evangelical resurgence of the 1950s and 1960s became fragmented.'

Always there were people urging CICCU to 'make the main thing the main thing', that particular comment coming in the years when the 'Toronto blessing' was much talked about. 'Keep the emphasis on a Christ-centred, cross-focused gospel and seek only to hold together those who are committed to that gospel as of first importance and to a desire to share it with others. There is a danger that, in trying to hold everyone together, we lose the focus that has been CICCU's great strength over the years. It must be possible to hold together charismatic and more conservative evangelicals – but only those who can distinguish between what is primary (i.e. Christ and his cross) and what is secondary (tongues, prophecy, etc.). Concentrate on the essentials: get those right and stick to them.' The need for discernment was always a stimulus to go back and search the Scriptures.

Trusting God

Another lesson that came home to many was the need to trust God. 'Never forget that it is the Lord's work. If you ever want to see a testimony to God's sustaining power, it is in the fact that in our universities the Christian flame burns brightly from the CUs, despite inexperienced leadership and the constant throughput of individuals.' Trusting God meant 'learning to please God, not people'. 'My responsibilities', another recalled, 'were far more demanding than I had expected and drove me to prayer. They challenged me about what in my faith was merely cultural and what biblical. I also felt the heartache of gospel ministry.' All this 'taught me dependence on God; I was utterly out of my depth'. 'I was forced to depend on Christ in what was a hard year and I matured as a Christian as a result. As I had been converted for only three years when I began, I had to grow fast – especially in doctrinal understanding.'

Faithful and clear

A further lesson that many took away was the need to be faithful to the Bible and clear in expressing its teaching. 'Don't assume the gospel. The term is bandied about and its meaning may be understood in different ways by different people. So it must be taught from the Bible, it must be held out to students who have not yet put their trust in the Lord Jesus and it must be lived out in our lives. If the CICCU is to last as an interdenominational group, its unity must be based on the gospel.'

As he was leaving office another passed this on passionately to those who were taking over: 'Read 2 Timothy 3:1 – 4:8. Do not be dismayed at sin and opposition – in the future, it seems to me, the work of evangelism will be increasingly hard and opposition will grow. But CICCU has at times in its history been very small and weak, yet God has used it. Be very firmly established in the Bible. Preach the word. Provide a clear lead. Fight the good fight, finish the race, live for heaven. Then I would read 2 Timothy 3:1 – 4:8 again and repeat those words.' He saw that the truth of the Christian life as 'the good fight' needed to be maintained lest CICCU's distinctive witness weaken. Throughout CICCU's 125 years there was always a battle for truth that called for vigilance and resolution.

Non-negotiable

For years CICCU was the only non-denominational evangelical student society in Cambridge and the largest religious society. CICCU members were more cohesive in their church background or affiliation and in their understanding of what 'evangelical' meant. Times changed

as Christians came into CICCU from a greater variety
of churches and brought a greater mix of church distinctives. The older sense of needing to stand or fight for truth
tended to fade as liberalism's influence ebbed away and
evangelical confidence grew. There was more opportunity
to follow sectional distinctives rather than a distinctive witness, with greater risk of diversion and division.

CICCU aimed to keep all evangelical students united
on a 'gospel priority, truths of first importance' basis, even
when some wanted to pursue other goals. It will take
renewed focus on the non-negotiable truths to preserve
that unity, so that the gospel that Cambridge and the
world so desperately needs may be clearly presented and
the vision kept bright of presenting Christ's claims to every
student.

Looking back,
looking forward

During its first quarter century the CICCU became relatively strong. It was *the* evangelical student society in the 1880s and 1890s and almost every undergraduate knew it and had met some of its members. The main crises of belief still lay ahead. The CICCU had not yet entered the twentieth century, when theological liberalism quickly ate into the evangelical belief of many. It had not then become aware of the doctrinal drift that led up to the crucial questions and the parting of friends in 1919.

At the CICCU's centenary in 1977 the position looked similar to the 1890s. The CICCU had the evangelical field more or less to itself. It involved around 1,000 undergraduates in its central and college-based activities. It had the ear of many who were not Christians and God was doing a significant work in many lives. It was united in essentials and on course for the gospel.

Two questions

The centenary story therefore posed two questions. First, what danger was there of the current generation repeating the mistake of the 1890s and allowing belief to drift? If the CICCU had grown prosperous, it would obviously be tempted to be less careful about its doctrinal stand, the identity of its witness and its aims. It was when all seemed successful in that earlier period that plausible but subtly divergent views began to undermine the gospel, leaving only a remnant to carry on the witness. Would that history be repeated?

And second: did the later generation have the evangelistic zeal of the earlier one? Did college groups still make sure that every fresher had the chance to talk over the claims of Christ? Did dangerous missionary service in remote places still capture some members' hearts? Did the CICCU still see itself as a task force for evangelizing in Cambridge, Britain and to the ends of the earth?

The account of the last twenty-five years shows that God remarkably preserved the CICCU's testimony. It was not diverted or distracted from its biblical base or its gospel aims, despite many influences in other directions. That is a matter for profound gratitude to God, not least for those who came into eternal life through the CICCU and its members.

Its continuance over 125 years is the more remarkable since it is a student work always led by young, sometimes very young, Christians. Most had previously had little or no comparable Christian responsibility. In that time, moreover, it had the annual turnover in its leadership. Yet by and large it avoided the drift and distractions that dragged so many movements and churches down. The work went on because students got their heads into the Bible and God's Spirit got his Word into their hearts. They received its clear message and lived to pass it on.

Truth, love, obedience

Under God they held together doctrine, devotion and morals. They grasped the connection between these three – between truth, love and the obedience that leads to both holy living and evangelism. They knew that, if anything cuts one of those three elements away from the others, then spiritual life and obedience will wither. They realized that God had spoken and that it is his truth – the Word of God, the word of the cross – that his Spirit uses to change people's minds and lives. They saw that what keeps people going in self-sacrifice and service is gratitude for what Christ suffered and achieved on the cross: 'Christ's love compels us, because we are convinced that one died for all' (2 Corinthians 5:14).

In the 125th year the work continued, but faced daunting challenges from secular culture and the influence it has on Christians. The temptations remained – to belief and convictions on the one hand and to life and standards on the other. Perhaps the major pressure is to shift the basis of belief and behaviour away from objective, revealed truth to subjective ideas and guidance. This is what happened when liberalism bowed to human reason. It was on that basis that the Student Christian Movement could give the atoning blood of Christ only 'a place' in their message, not the central place it has in the Bible. But the CICCU would not be wooed to a broader 'Christianity' in 1919 or since, not even by the flattering but false prospect of exerting greater influence on a wider stage.

In the period up to 1920 most observers found it acutely disappointing that a movement with the evangelistic and missionary tradition of the CICCU seemed to turn its back on the opportunity of influencing the really big, worldwide and powerful movement that the SCM had become. The CICCU seemed a mere backwater. But the fact that it did turn away from that was the reason why the witness continued. The CICCU was even willing to face a drop in numbers if that were the price of not compromising God's priorities for the gospel. It may have to face that decision again.

A similar danger arose in the late 1920s and 1930s when the Moral Rearmament movement appeared on the scene. That presented a choice between 'orthodoxy and life', the one dry, the other vibrant. Its appeal lay in the question 'Why cling to orthodoxy if the MRA Groups offered life?' It replaced study of the Bible as the given Word of God with times of 'listening to God' with the mind blank and a pencil and paper to hand. Despite this superspiritual appeal, its influence waned and the CICCU in the end saw it for what it was and turned away from its subjectivism. In both those episodes the CICCU, in fellowship with the other CUs and the IVF/UCCF, hammered out a policy: cooperation with bodies that do not have the same witness is inconsistent, because harmful to the clarity and author-ity of the gospel, and ultimately unfruitful.

Looking elsewhere

One main temptation for the CICCU today is similar: not to deny the Bible as the Word of God, but to put the focus elsewhere in practice and ministry. It can seem super-spiritual to bypass the objective Word and rely on direct words from God. Sometimes truth can slip in the pursuit of diversity. Sometimes the surrounding culture can skew the message and blunt its point. Sometimes subjectivism leads to a gospel-plus, imposing extra experiences or demands in addition to the gospel's clear but costly 'repent and believe'.

This is why the CICCU maintained the wholesome tra-dition of expounding and explaining the Bible. It wanted its teaching to keep as close as possible to the Holy Spirit's intention through the original author. It took this approach because it reduced dependence on the personal ideas of any teacher and let the Bible speak. As this was vital for evangelism and the whole Christian life, the CICCU also encouraged college CICCU groups to do

Bible study, since getting at the meaning of the text meant listening to God's voice. Such teaching laid the foundation for whatever testings might come. As Helen Roseveare said, it is God's Word that will help and hold a Christian in front of a firing squad.

The CICCU generally maintained a love for biblical doctrine, not least because it fed evangelism. Foundational here was the biblical teaching on why Christ died – to give himself as our substitute, to turn away the wrath of God we so fully deserved. The wrong kind of doctrinal interest can certainly be distracting, but not one that keeps its focus on the cross. Moreover, the CICCU found that evangelism will dry up if its roots in biblical truth are not continually watered. An evangelizing agency like the CICCU needed constant biblical feeding, correction, nurture and stimulus if it were to keep on track, avoid diversions and not become formulaic or simplistic.

This is why the CICCU always wanted to be clear on the nature and content of the gospel. It was always important to note what other approaches were *not* saying, as well as what they were saying. Many true things could be included, but if the saving truths were not kept central, the message would become defective and attention would turn to peripheral things. Many true things, for example, might be said about the gospel giving fulfilment and purpose, or about its implications for social concern – things with which no Christian could disagree. But if the message did not focus on the atoning blood of Christ and why he needed to die; if it did not speak of God's wrath as well as his love, judgment as well as grace, sin as well as new life, then it would sell its hearers short.

This biblical emphasis steered the CICCU away from intellectualism and doctrinal aridity on the one hand and from subjectivism and superspirituality on the other. At the same time the CICCU encouraged thoughtful engagement between biblical thinking and the intellectual, social and ethical issues of the day. It was aware of the need for the Christian mind to develop. This was important in itself as well as for evangelism, for it saved converts from indulging in private experiences and set them on the way to obeying Christ in the wider world. For this reason good Christian reading has always been encouraged.

Power in the message

These factors helped the CICCU to continue thoughtful and doctrinally contentful evangelism – teaching or proclamation evangelism. This was a largely new approach in John Stott's early missions, but it became widely accepted and was the instrument of many conversions. The CICCU adapted its form and packaging to meet students as their culture changed, but the fundamental convictions remained the same: that the gospel *message* is God's power to save everyone who believes (Romans 1:16). The three different missions based on New Testament Gospels were variants of this approach. However, those convictions constantly needed reinforcement, since other approaches could make evangelism wholly or essentially 'relational' or 'small group' rather than message-based and could put 'belonging before believing'. On their own such approaches could downplay the message and deprive people of the chance to hear the gospel.

For years the CICCU was the main or only body for evangelical students in Cambridge. CICCU members were more cohesive in terms of their church background or affiliation and their views of what evangelical meant. Times have changed. CICCU members now come from a wider range of churches, bringing with them a greater mix of church distinctives. Christian students face more opportunity to follow denominational or sectional distinctives, with a greater risk of diversion or division. This is particularly the case where there seems less awareness of the need to fight for core truth. But the New Testament shows that it is never safe to let our defences down and that we always need discernment.

The CICCU will therefore constantly have to work at holding together evangelicals from various backgrounds, but only on a 'gospel priority, truths of first importance' basis. One recurring theme in the CICCU story is that unity must never be sought if it blurs, dilutes or adds to the gospel in the process; some truths are non-negotiable and cannot be compromised. True unity is both as broad and as narrow as the gospel. Each new CICCU generation needs to renew its focus on those truths if it is to preserve the unity and clarity in the gospel that Cambridge desperately needs. But if God has spoken, none who follows him needs to fear.

The golden thread

In the face of these pressures, what is the golden thread that runs through the CICCU's life, providing continuity and consistency? The single thread that has been present in all periods is constant exposure to the Bible. Under God, that is what has kept the CICCU alive and true to the gospel. The personal quiet times with God, the college Bible studies, the central Bible Readings (later called Bible Teachings) and the Bible-based evangelistic events – these have exposed the CICCU's members to a consistent flow of biblical input and application. Through the ever-new and life-giving spring of his Word God's Spirit has often refreshed people, turning them from indifference or dry orthodoxy to spiritual reality and true love for God. Future members of the CICCU need equally to be fed on the Bible so that they will be able to stand when the pressures mount.

For many years the CICCU Missionary Prayer Card

carried the words of Revelation 12:11, 'They overcame him by the blood of the Lamb and by the word of their testimony; they did not love their lives so much as to shrink from death.' May that always be true so that, having done all, the CICCU will stand firm (Ephesians 6:13).

The concluding perspective on these 125 years comes from Psalm 103:15–18 and 1 Peter 1:24–25:

> As for man, his days are like grass,
>   he flourishes like a flower of the field;
> the wind blows over it and it is gone,
>   and its place remembers it no more.
> But from everlasting to everlasting
>   the LORD's love is with those who fear him,
>   and his righteousness with their children's children –
> with those who keep his covenant
>   and remember to obey his precepts.

> For you have been born again, not of perishable seed, but of imperishable, through the living and enduring word of God. For,

> 'All men are like grass,
>   and all their glory is like the flowers of the field;
> the grass withers and the flowers fall,
>   but the word of the Lord stands for ever.'

> And this is the word that was preached to you.

Notes

Chapter 1

1 The Cambridge University Act of 1856 (effective 1858) allowed students to enrol, hold scholarships and take BA degrees without religious tests. It was still necessary, however, to agree to the Thirty-nine Articles of the Church of England in order to be an MA or hold any office. All university teachers were therefore still members of the Church of England. In 1871, by the University Tests Act, religious tests were removed from all lay offices (the divinity faculty staff, therefore, remained Anglican). King's College London, and Durham University were also strongly Anglican and the latter was not freed from tests until this 1871 Act. University College London was a 'secular' foundation supported by many Nonconformists as well as Jeremy Bentham and his friends. To put this in its more human context, Oliver Barclay's paternal grandfather had to go to University College London rather than to Oxford or Cambridge, where friends and relatives were, because he was a Quaker and as a matter of principle did not feel free to sign the Articles.

2 We shall use the word 'evangelical' in this book in the

sense in which it is generally used in Britain. See *Evangelism In Britain 1935–1955: A Personal Sketch* by O. R. Barclay (IVP, 1997); *Ultimate Realities* (an exposition of the UCCF's doctrinal basis) by Bob Horn (IVP, 1999); and the earlier *Christ the Controversialist* by J. R. W. Stott (IVP, 1990) with its introductory essay B.

In other countries 'evangelical' sometimes carries a different sense, but here it refers to those who emphasize the reliability and final authority of the Bible (over reason, tradition, the church, etc.) and whose message focuses on the finished work of Christ on the cross for our forgiveness, so that we cannot add to what he has done by works, rituals or spiritual earnestness. It can be characterized in the phrase 'by Christ alone, through faith alone, from Scripture alone'.

3 In Simeon's time and nearly up to the Second World War, there was a sharp divide between the undergraduates and the senior members of the university. The latter expected to be treated with considerable respect as the leaders of the university and thought of themselves as forming the minds of the young. There were few who came in between. This book refers to the latter as 'the seniors'. At this stage they were mostly members of teaching staff who held a 'fellowship' (which was for life) in one of the colleges and dined at a college high table. The teaching staff were popularly called 'dons' and, since dons were all single and lived in college, the word 'donnish' has become a synonym for academic eccentricity. The nearest equivalent phrase, perhaps, is 'the absent-minded professor'. Today college fellowships are no longer held for life and most fellows are married and live out of college. There is also now a large group of research students and other graduate students who dine with the undergraduates. This was chiefly, however, a post-1939 development.

4 Simeon started with William Law's *The Whole Duty of Man*. This was the only religious book he knew of and it started the process in his mind. Bishop Thomas Wilson's *A Short and Plain Instruction for the Lord's Supper* (1733) brought him to assurance of salvation through faith in the substitutionary death of Christ.

5 A student who had come to scoff was heard to say, on leaving the church, ' "Well, Simeon is no fool however!" "Fool!" replied his companion, "did you ever hear such a sermon before?" ' (H. C. G. Moule, *Charles Simeon* [1892; reissued IVP, 1948], p. 64).

6 They were pupils at the school called Liverpool College. Both had been influenced by the widespread religious revival of 1859, which had deeply affected the churches in America and all over Britain.

7 Girton College for women was started in 1869 with five students at Hitchin, 27 miles away. In 1873 it was moved to Girton Village, very properly nearly two miles outside Cambridge! Newnham College started in Cambridge in 1871, also with five students. In 1873 the first three women (from Girton) took the degree examination and passed, but women were not fully members of the university until 1948. Up to that point 'members of the University and of the Women's Colleges' was the phrase to be used to include both men and women. University education for women was regarded as very avant-garde at that time.

8 The Brethren movement began in Dublin in the late 1820s and spread quickly to England. In its early days it drew a great deal of its support from the upper middle class and in this respect differed from some other forms of nineteenth-century Nonconformity. By the time the CICCU was founded a definite Brethren association had been built up in a number of such families. Since it was customary for children from

these homes to go to university, Brethren ideas soon made themselves felt in the CICCU in spite of the very strong Anglican influence. There were soon also some Quakers in the CICCU for similar reasons. The president in 1900, for instance, was a Quaker and several others were from Quaker stock, though now members of the Church of England.

9 See J. C. Pollock, *The Cambridge Seven* (IVP, 1955), p. 26. Waldegrave was the son of the evangelical peer Lord Radstock who, while he himself never broke his links with the Church of England, was an accepted speaker and leader among the Brethren. Robert Armitage's comment was a verbal one made to the author in about 1950. Armitage became MP for Leeds.

10 S. A. Blackwood, a civil servant, later Sir Arthur Blackwood, head of the Post Office.

11 This was a conference by invitation of William Cowper-Temple, MP (author of the influential Cowper-Temple Clause on Religious Education) at his large country house at Broadlands, Hampshire.

12 Even in 1898 there were only three officers who formed a sort of unofficial executive committee. The rest of the business was settled by the meeting of college reps. This seems to have been very infrequent. They all met individually, of course, from time to time at the DPM. It was not until 1910 that a more formal executive committee was elected by the college reps' meeting, which became the general committee.

13 The Cambridge colleges were then fairly small communities, most of only about 100 students. Nearly everyone lived in College. There were a few non-collegiate students who could not afford college fees (these later formed Fitzwilliam House, which in due course became a full college of the university). In 1977 there were 25 colleges, the largest being Trinity College with

226 From Cambridge to the World

750 undergraduates and over 200 graduate students. In 2002 Cambridge has 31 colleges.

In the 1870s many colleges had a distinctive character; King's, for instance, contained largely Old Etonians. Trinity (not to be confused with either a smaller college, Trinity Hall, or with Holy Trinity Church) had a good many aristocrats and was also the centre of advance in physics. Caius had a reputation for medicine. It was therefore a significant step to get every college of the university represented.

Chapter 2

14 G. M. Davies, *A Chaplain in India* (Marshall, Morgan and Scott, 1933). Davies went to Cambridge in 1878 as a non-collegiate student for the first year, because his father was an impecunious parson. His total expenses for fees and board and lodging for that year were £63 1s. 7d.

15 Up to the 1940s undergraduates and BAs had to wear an academic gown and mortarboard ('cap and gown') outside college after dark. They could thereby be distinguished, at a glance, by townspeople and senior members of the university. If a proctor met any undergraduate breaking this rule, he would take the student's name and address and impose a fine of 6s. 8d. (a third of a pound). Proctors were, and are, the disciplinary officers of the university.

16 Buxton was brought along by his father. He was at the time a recent graduate but, like many others, especially prominent sportsmen (he had played tennis for the university), he had kept up some links with university life. He came from a truly Christian background but was not, up to this point, personally trusting Christ. This was typical of many sons of evangelical families who were helped in the Mission.

Buxton later became a leading missionary in Japan.

17 The Backs are the large area of grass and trees behind the colleges and bordering the river Cam.

18 Quoted in E. S. Woods and F. B. MacNutt, *Theodore, Bishop of Winchester: A Memoir of Frank Theodore Woods 1874–1932* (SPCK, 1933). The references to 'Woods' are to Theodore Woods (see pp. 39, 98).

19 Woods and MacNutt, *Theodore, Bishop of Winchester*, p. 16.

20 Moule was appointed Norrisian Professor of Divinity after he had been Principal of Ridley Hall. The move to Ridley (not a step up academically) represented his concern with, and gifts for, pastoral rather than merely academic theology, and from then on he ceased to do much battle in the increasingly critical and arid theological world, though he wrote excellent commentaries.

Chapter 3

21 See Pollock, *The Cambridge Seven*, and N. P. Grubb, *C. T. Studd: Cricketer and Pioneer* (Lutterworth Press, 1933).

22 Eugene Stock, *The History of the Church Missionary Society* (CMS, 1899), vol. II, pp. 46–47, and vol. III, pp. 33–34 and 354. The CIM records do not tell us which of their missionaries had been at Cambridge.

23 The earliest basis (1886) was, 'We are willing and desirous, God permitting, to become foreign missionaries.' At Moody's Mount Hermon conference in 1886, where Wilder and his sister had prayed for 100 volunteers, exactly 100 signed that declaration. See R. P. Wilder, *The Student Volunteer Movement* (SVM, 1938). The American movement was called 'The Student Volunteer Movement for Foreign Missions' and the British 'The Student Volunteer Missionary Union'.

24 R. P. Wilder, *The Great Commission* (Oliphants, 1936),
     p. 46. Cambridge had already sent notable missionar-
     ies abroad, of whom Henry Martyn was the most
     famous.

25 Much of this chapter is culled from Tissington Tatlow's
     official account, *The Story of the Student Christian
     Movement of Great Britain and Ireland* (SCM Press,
     1933), especially chs 2, 3 and 4. See in particular pp.
     48–62 and see ch. 5 for the Liverpool conference. See
     also R. P. Wilder's books.

26 Basil Matthews in his biography *John R. Mott, World
     Citizen* (SCM Press, 1934), p. 165, quoted a Cam-
     bridge student describing his 1908 visit: 'The meeting
     on the fourth night (of a six-day mission) defies de-
     scription. It seems to belong to the land of dreams and
     impossibilities . . . 1,250 present . . . An after meeting
     was held at which 560 remained; never before have we
     seen University men jumping over forms to secure
     good seats at an after meeting.'

27 The 1897 diary of the CICCU president (D. B. Bar-
     clay) describes his life both before and after he took of-
     fice. His day included an average of six hours' work
     (study) six days a week. This was meticulously record-
     ed so as to ensure that he reached the target. He usu-
     ally worked all morning and then attended the DPM
     before lunch. There was occasional squash or tennis in
     the afternoon and an hour or two walking or cycling
     with friends (often tandem and once a trip up the St
     Neots Road on a friend's motor tricycle). There was
     constant entertaining of a group of a dozen or so
     friends, and frequent callers and calls on people con-
     cerned with the CICCU, including G. T. Manley, then
     a fellow, and the two ordained members of the Cam-
     bridge Pastorate (Dodderidge and Armitage). It was
     usual to have friends to breakfast, lunch and tea, or to

go out for these meals. Sunday included College Chapel (attendance was compulsory twice during the week as well as on Sunday), a prayer meeting for old boys of his school, sometimes a college Bible study run by senior men, the CICCU sermon (150–300 present) followed by a squash with the same speaker (usually 25 or so present), or in the summer an Open-air on Parker's Piece instead of both. This, however, left time for reading and a walk! He did not teach in a Sunday school, perhaps because he had been Secretary of the CMU and was responsible for the CICCU/OICCU Conference before be joined the executive committee. He often attended CMU meetings. There was no CICCU activity at the college level, so that the DPM and Sunday activities were the main term-time activities. In addition were the warm, stimulating friendships and the informal prayer and sometimes Bible study which were a normal item in their tea parties and evening discussions. Vacation conferences also played their part.

28 Tatlow, *The Story of the Student Christian Movement*, p. 33.

29 E.g. Professor E. T. Whittaker, quoted in Woods and MacNutt, *Theodore, Bishop of Winchester*, pp. 16, 25. See also their comments about Theodore Woods.

Chapter 4

30 Tatlow, *The Story of the Student Christian Movement*, pp. 220, 272.

31 See, e.g., pp. 36–37 of the third edition (1891): 'It is inconceivable that the Israelites should have brought with them out of the desert a cultus they observed in the time of the kings (Exodus 22, 23 and 24), which throughout presupposed the fields and gardens of Palestine; they borrowed it from the Canaanites.' See also

pp. 21, 53. That could be called unscholarly specula-
tion dressed up in a dogmatic assertion. At the time it
was thought to be very scientific and scholarly by all but
a few. Basically it was not 'rational' – it did not follow
reasonably and necessarily from the actual data. It im-
posed upon the Bible its own criteria of what seemed
reasonable to the modern mind and ignored those data
that did not fit in. As time went on that left less and less
of biblical truth still to be believed.

This *rationalistic* approach makes 'what seems reasonable to me and my circle' the final test of what shall
be accepted. Reason is made into a bed of Procrustes –
Procrustes was that unsavoury character of Greek
mythology whose guests were either stretched out to
the full length of his bed or else cut down so that they
fitted it exactly.

A *rational* approach may mean, however, the very
opposite of that – a sitting under the facts to make sure
that our reasoning follows faithfully from whatever
data we have been given. In this sense science is rational but not rationalistic. The approach of Wellhausen and the higher critics generally was rationalistic
and therefore to modern eyes seems unscientific and
unscholarly in the strict sense of those terms. It was,
however, immensely attractive because it fitted the
Bible into the popular philosophical framework by
cutting out the points that did not match and finding
plausible reasons for doing so, as in the quotation
above. It was believed that it would make it easier for
people to accept the message of the Bible.

Many evangelicals (and others) overreacted and became hostile to any use of reason or scholarly study of
the Bible. They forgot that while reason is fallen, so are
all our other faculties. If reasoning is kept in its proper
place as a humble tool to understand God-given data,

we are meant to use it as part of being human in God's image – in contrast to purely emotional, speculative or claimed imaginative approaches to the Bible under the guidance of the Holy Spirit.

Lower criticism (which includes much scholarly textual criticism) must not be confused with higher criticism. By lower criticism is usually meant the attempt to discover the best text and its exact meaning without any 'higher critical' principle to control the results.

32 Canon Charles Smyth in a lecture at Cambridge. He also stressed the damage to the spirit of evangelicals from the lawsuits in which they became involved when they tried to exclude ritualistic practices. The second point, however, hardly applied to Cambridge.

33 See Tatlow, *The Story of the Student Christian Movement*.

34 SCM archives, Birmingham: letter dated 8 October 1910 to Miss E. A. Constable, a student at the Royal Free Hospital who wrote objecting to what Peake had said at the conference.

35 By 1918 the CMS committee was also sharply divided and in 1922 even the CMS itself (although broadly evangelical) lost a substantial group of missionaries and supporters to form the new Bible Churchmen's Missionary Society. It is interesting that several of the older CICCU stalwarts, including G. T. Manley, did not join the BCMS, although they were upset by what was happening in the CMS. They believed that there was need for a far tougher policy in the student world than they felt was essential in some church contexts.

36 John R. Mott was very emphatic about leaving Keswick. See SCM archives.

37 SCM archives: letter from F. H. Mosse, dated 28 January 1912.

38 Mother SCM, however, was also becoming more in-
    terested in the social application of Christianity than in
    missionary study or evangelistic work. This question is
    discussed in chapter 6. Some, like Wilder, believed that
    this was a cause of decline; others believed it was rather
    a result of losing the biblical priorities. In any case, stu-
    dents in the SCM were being led by their senior
    friends into increasingly sophisticated social studies
    and the CICCU held back.

39 The Mission is described in n. 26, above.

40 Morris became a missionary bishop of North Africa.
    Mowll became, first, a bishop in China and then
    Archbishop of Sydney. Mowll was president of the
    CICCU for five terms and exerted a strong influence
    until ordination in 1913. His ordination, however,
    was blocked by the Bishop of Ely who refused to
    license him when he was invited to be curate of
    Holy Trinity Church, Cambridge. This was almost
    certainly because of his uncompromising stand, as
    there was no other apparent reason. He then went to
    Wycliffe College, Toronto, and later to China. See
    Marcus Loane's biography, which has a full account of
    the whole Cambridge period from Mowll's point of
    view.

Chapter 5

41 Verbal communication with R. L. Pelly before he died
    in 1976 confirmed this. Ben Harder obtained an inter-
    view (see 'Chief sources').

42 If this sounds conceited about the influence of Cam-
    bridge, it must be remembered that it was, for a long
    time, a cause of complaint by others that nearly all the
    influential posts in the Church of England were held
    by Oxford or Cambridge men. They were influential
    out of all proportion to their numbers and they also

still provided, between them, a large majority of the ordinands for the Church of England ministry. Oxford and Cambridge graduates also provided important lay leadership in many of the professions. It was only after the Second World War that this situation was totally changed.

43 For instance, the evangelical societies working in South America were excluded from the 1910 Edinburgh Missionary Conference as a condition laid down by certain High Church leaders for their attendance at it. See also n. 40 above.

44 See Tatlow, *The Story of the Student Christian Movement*, p. 486. The new Basis read, 'In joining this union I declare my faith in God through Jesus Christ, whom as Saviour and Lord I desire to serve.' Of the delegates at the SCM General Committee 364 voted in favour and 28 against.

45 Although they were not using it, the SCM wished to retain the title LICCU for London when evangelical groups were re-formed there. So the title London Inter-Faculty Christian Union (LIFCU) was used instead.

46 This was published by Marshall, Morgan and Scott and was only thirty-five pages long. The text was signed (initials only) by six CICCU leaders including the first three presidents since disaffiliation. Handley Moule, who was by then Bishop of Durham, wrote a foreword.

47 Howard Mowll made this comment from personal knowledge of the men. See Marcus Loane's biography.

48 Some who would not speak of Christ's deity spoke of his 'divinity', but meant far less than that he was God. At the conference in 1906 some students had been shocked by a speaker who would go no further than to say that Jesus 'has to us the value of Deity' (verbal

communication from Mrs G. R. Barclay, née Watney).
49 Oliver Tomkins, *The Life of Edward Woods* (SCM Press, 1957), p. 56.
50 Ibid., p. 56. Edward Woods wrote in 1921, 'Whatever else is obscure to me, this then I am beginning at least to see with absolute clearness, and that is that Christianity is really intended to provide a glowing comprehensive fellowship for all who can call Jesus Lord and slave for His Kingdom.'
51 Memorandum by Norman P. Grubb.

Chapter 6

52 Woods and MacNutt, *Theodore, Bishop of Winchester*, p. 132.
53 The Union Society in Cambridge was the Debating Society and club, with restaurant and library, and was not automatically joined by students as in most other universities. The president in 1926 was A. M. Ramsey (later Archbishop of Canterbury).
54 C. B. Raven, *The Wanderers' Way* (1928). In spite of his aggressive liberalism Raven had extraordinary charm and influence. The following is one of the many stories told about Charles Raven: 'When rehearsing for a certain great occasion F. W. Dwelly (the Dean) became aware of the need for colour in a certain blank area of the [Liverpool] Cathedral. "What we need over there," he exclaimed, "is a splash of colour. You, Charles, in your chaplain's red cassock are just what we want. Please go and stand over there." To which Charles's answer is supposed to have been: "I was not aware, Mr. Dean, that when I was ordained to the sacred ministry it was in order to be a splash of colour in any situation."' From F. W. Dillistone, *Charles Raven* (Hodder and Stoughton, 1975), p. 144.
55 H. Earnshaw Smith (1923–6, part-time), Hugh R.

Gough (1927), Norman Grubb (1929) and Kenneth Hooker (1929–30).

56 *A Brief History of the Inter-Varsity Fellowship of Evangelical Christian Unions* (IVFECU, no date, but evidently late 1928), pp. 27, 9, 19.

57 The Inter-Varsity Conference was held annually from 1919 onwards and each year appointed a committee to plan the next one and a secretary who, from 1924 onwards, was Douglas Johnson. In 1928 this conference created the Inter-Varsity Fellowship of Evangelical Christian Unions, with thirteen universities affiliated – Aberdeen, Belfast, Bristol, Cambridge (men's and women's CUs), Cardiff, Dublin (men's and women's CUs), Edinburgh, Glasgow, Liverpool, London, Manchester, Oxford and St Andrews. See *A Brief History of the IVFECU*. Douglas Johnson was Secretary of the IVF until 1964. He always denied that he had any serious influence, but all those who benefited from his friendship and counsel knew otherwise.

58 Cambridge University Missionary Band letter, 28 August 1922.

Chapter 7

59 His mother and then his sister also helped to provide admirable Sunday teas and other hospitality at their house in Grange Road. Many humorous Basil At. stories were still in circulation years later; but the fact that he was the subject of so many jokes made his overwhelmingly strong views bearable and wholesome.

60 This was me [ORB], and I did not take the advice given!

61 This was Derek Kidner (later Warden of Tyndale House). He had studied music in London and was a skilled performer. He came up to Cambridge to read theology. The CICCU were delighted when their

president was the performer at a public concert in the Guildhall and even more delighted when he got a first-class degree in theology. He represented and, to his own generation, set the example of a more positive attitude to theology. John Wenham, who had graduated in 1935, was a fairly frequent visitor trying to stir up the TSF and to help individuals. Each generation needed fresh leaders in this relatively new trend and John Wenham tried to spot the men who could do it and to encourage them both at Cambridge and elsewhere. He constantly lent and gave important books to students, to their great benefit.

62 Sir Frederick Catherwood had no interest in such subjects while he was an undergraduate. Later he brought together a group of evangelicals to write papers which eventually made a ground-breaking book, *The Christian in Industrial Society* (IVP, 1964). The group turned out to consist almost entirely of old CICCU men then in industry. His subsequent books, particularly *The Christian Citizen* (Hodder and Stoughton, 1969), also contributed substantially to the discussion in a constructive and biblical way.

Chapter 8

63 The moving spirit behind this was Bishop Stephen Neill, who was then Chaplain of Trinity College. He had been, in turn, on both the CICCU and SCM committees in the 1920s and, though very much in sympathy with the CICCU's theology, he could never quite appreciate the need for the distinctive witness of the CICCU.

64 The first edition of *Basic Christianity* (IVP, 1958) was longer and more solid than the revised edition (IVP, 1971). It has been translated into fifty-two languages and has sold well over a quarter of a million copies in

its English editions. Of all the evangelistic books that IVP have published, this was the one that most frequently brought letters telling of conversions through it.

65 Almost every college had on its staff both a dean of chapel (often a theologian of ability with teaching and other responsibilities) and a chaplain, who was a younger ordained man entrusted with the welfare of students and pastoral functions. Some colleges had more than one chaplain. Inevitably the chaplains liked to spend time with the CICCU members and sought to have some influence in areas where they thought the CICCU needed help. At this time most chaplains were somewhat liberal High Churchmen; only two or three were evangelical.

66 Basil F. C. Atkinson, 'Basil's Recollections' (handwritten memorandum, 1966).

Chapter 9

67 These letters were reprinted as a pamphlet and published by *The Times* under the title *Fundamentalism: A Religious Problem* (Times Publishing, 1955).

68 The article was in *The Bishopric* of February 1965, pp. 24–26. To quote more fully, 'It offers authority and security, quick and sure, to a generation restless and insecure. Other and more wholesome versions of Christianity offer security indeed – but rather more slowly: the security of growing gradually into the spiritual life of the Church, or the security of bringing a thoughtful and honest mind to rest upon the verities of the Christian faith. But here is security – in a single night. Hither, young man: drown your worries in the rapture of conversion: stifle your doubts by abdicating the use of your mind. A rousing sermon, a hurricane of emotion, a will to leap in the dark – and peace at once

and for ever ... He (Billy Graham) has gone. Our English fundamentalism remains. It is *heretical*, in one of the classic meanings of heresy, in that it represents a fixation of distorted elements from the Bible without the balanced tradition of scriptural truth as a whole. It is *sectarian*, in that the ardent fundamentalist has no regard for religion outside his own experience and vocabulary ... It is time that there was more perception of our true Anglican vocation in theology – to follow the "threefold cord" of Scripture, Tradition and Reason and to withstand the bibliolatrists as stoutly as Hooker withstood the Puritans of his day.

'For the evangelist, there is no golden key. It must be a simple gospel, without sophistication. It must be a gospel which speaks of sin and judgment, with a call for decision. But it must present Christ Himself and not a theory about Him which His apostles did not really teach; and Christ as present in the Sacraments wherein His touch still has its power. It must evoke the response not only of the will and the emotions, but also of the mind. The convert is not called upon to be an "intellectual"; he is called upon not to stifle his mind but to allow Christ to open it to a new service of God and his fellows. The Church must pray that men will be raised up with the power so to preach, that the stream of conversions will not be followed by a backwash of moral casualties and disillusioned sceptics.'

69 Some people have thought that the title 'High Church' refers to a person's status in the Church of England! That is totally wrong. The High Church tradition in the nineteenth century was proud to take a 'high' view of the Church of England and its sacraments. This was in contrast to either the Low Church view (mainly, but by no means entirely, evangelical) or the Broad Church (moderate) emphases. Some older High Church lead-

ers were practically Lutheran and had much in common with evangelicals on the essentials, often standing together against the Broad Church party.

As the nineteenth century progressed, however, the High Church party became increasingly influenced by Roman Catholic theology. Some of this group, often called Anglo-Catholics, accepted almost the whole of Roman theology, except the authority of the pope. By 1900 most of them were also more or less influenced by a liberal attitude to the Bible and so fell back on church tradition (and to some extent reason) as a basis for the faith. By the 1950s the normal High Church approach was, as Bishop Ramsey put it in his article in *The Bishopric*, an appeal to 'follow the "threefold cord" of Scripture, Tradition and Reason' in which Reason (note the capital letters) had increasingly the final word (see quote in n. 68 above). Most believed that you became a Christian by baptism and grew up as a Christian by attendance at Communion and the other ritual ordinances of the church. Ramsey typically disliked any idea of abrupt conversion and wanted people to grow 'gradually into the spiritual life of the Church'. The opposition to evangelical teaching was therefore based broadly on a very different view of Christian truth and life. The situation in the High Church party, however, became rather fluid and the views which had been characteristic earlier (e.g. their attitude to baptism) were not always so strongly held later.

70 *York Journal of Convocation*, May 1957, pp. 92–93. The theological position of the speaker may be judged by the fact that he ended his speech by saying, 'I do not think there will ever be a revival of great religion until there has been a revival of great poetry.' He was seconding a resolution to receive a report on education

which included a jumble of accusations about 'uncritical fundamentalism' as 'sponsored in general by the Inter-Varsity Fellowship and by the Christian Unions'. Among 'characteristic views' were listed such a view of the church as led 'even to the extent of boycotting the college chapel; a radical view of the penal atonement, together with a rejection of baptismal regeneration and indifference to Holy Communion; intolerant individualism; a negative attitude to morals [*sic*] . . . 'Perhaps that last phrase was meant to refer to social ethics, but since it was general it was taken to be more sinister in its implications. Even at the time of the controversy it was hard to take some of these points seriously. In retrospect, since few later liberals were so wedded to the church as an institution, or to College Chapel, to baptismal regeneration or to strictly New Testament ethics, the criticism seems wide of the mark.

71 In 1962 the SCM Press published *A Survey of Christianity in the Universities*, based on figures for 1961–2. By then the Cambridge Methodist Society membership was down to 300 and the total national membership of Methodist societies was 2,000. Membership of the 18 Baptist societies was 650 and the 18 Congregational and Presbyterian societies 350. This survey gives IVF membership as 3,000 in the universities, and SCM 3,700, including 400 at Cambridge. In the 1940s the Methodist Society at Cambridge had claimed to have nearly 1,000 members.

72 Before the Second World War the more strongly re-formed independent churches and the Pentecostal churches tended not to encourage their young people to go to universities. If they did go, it was usually to a local university and not to Oxford or Cambridge.

73 The smaller college groups with no strong prayer fellowship of their own had been the backbone of the

DPM in this lean time. They valued it as some of the larger groups did not.

Chapter 10

74 Many challenges arise when attempting to write up very recent history:

The most obvious is that of attaining objectivity, particularly on any current or controversial issues. When events are still close, and so many people remember or took part in them, focus and assessments are not easy. The coverage of 1977–2002 is therefore interim rather than final. The perspective will doubtless be more objective in 2027 at the CICCU's 150th anniversary (which will also be the bicentenary of the start of the Jesus Lane Sunday School). Only when the Lord Jesus Christ returns will the full story be known.

Then there is the question of whom to mention or quote – or not. With so many contributing to the story, it is clearly impossible to name all those quoted. In the end I deemed it invidious, with only rare exceptions, to cite people by name. For everyone quoted, many more equally worthy or interesting people could also have been included. In any case, to pepper a short account with endless names would make tedious reading. Instead, I have tried to provide representative quotations and illustrations; readers from particular periods may have fun putting names to quotes. As a check on balance and accuracy, an unusually large number of readers saw and corrected the manuscript – both insiders and observers; but if the quotations given in three short chapters are insufficiently nuanced or comprehensive, the fault is mine [RMH].

Another problem comes from the constraints of space. A choice had to be made between basing the account on chronology or on themes. Chapters 10 to 12 take the latter course, covering different topics in the CICCU's life and work in that quarter century. They are therefore more an overview than a chronicle.

More records are available about the CICCU's policies, programmes and leaders than about its members; the average member did not put down lasting records of his or her experiences and decisions – as Execs did in the detailed minutes and bulging files of letters and papers.

75 Risto Lehtonen, *Story of a Storm: The Ecumenical Student Movement in the Turmoil of Revolution 1968 to 1973* (Eerdmans, 1998), pp. xi, xv-xvi, 339.

Chapter 11

76 Fusion's published material describes cells as having three elements: 'Love God, Love one another and Love the world (focus outwards)'. It 'wants evangelism to be ongoing, not based around "evangelistic events" but around lifestyle of reaching out to others. With this in mind, social engagement and social action play a vital role in the cells.' The framework for a cell meeting is 'Welcome, Worship, Word and Witness'.

77 *Extremism and Intolerance on Campus: CVCP Management Guidance Guidelines.* A report by the Committee of Vice-Chancellors and Principals (now called 'The voice of the universities'), 1998, ISBN 1 84036 013 5. This official report arose 'in the light of universities' experience of extremism and intolerance in recent years to consider freedom of speech provisions and codes of student discipline'. Its 'general principles' include:

2.0 Commitment 'to the principles of free enquiry and of free speech within the law';

2.1 'Vigorous debate is perfectly proper and acceptable and universities must therefore be tolerant of a wide range of views and opinions on social, economic, political and religious issues, however unorthodox, unpopular, uncomfortable, controversial or provocative'.

On Students' Unions it states:

12.3 The report requires 'a procedure for allocating resources to groups or clubs which is fair and set down in writing. Unions must exhibit conspicuous fairness and tolerance in relation to societies; however offensive may be the particular aims or policies, they have every right to exist and function.'

12.4 'It should not be permissible for a resolution to be tabled and debated which sought to limit the right of a group of students to exist and function within the union solely on account of its views or policies.'

12.6 'We urge all university governing bodies and students' unions to ensure that all groups of students which are conducting themselves properly and lawfully enjoy the full protection of the institution.'

12.8 'We think it may be reasonable for some clubs or societies to have restricted eligibility, say on religious or nationality grounds. Otherwise, it would be open to a group hostile to the club or society to join and take it over in a way that would be quite wrong.'

'Draft model clauses for Students' Unions' should include

3 'No group shall be denied the right to organize themselves within the Union on the grounds of their views, beliefs, policies or objectives. No existing club shall be disestablished or subject to particular restrictions on account of its members' views, beliefs, policies or objectives.'

6 'It shall be permissible for particular clubs or societies to impose restrictions on eligibility to join or participate on such grounds as national origins, ethnicity, religion, gender or sexual orientation.'

From the DfEE's *A Guide to Student Unions*, 1994, on 'Freedom of Speech':

28 'Section 43 of the Education (No. 2) Act 1986 requires universities and colleges to take such steps as are reasonably practicable to ensure freedom of speech within the law for students, employers and visiting speakers. This involves seeing that the use of premises (including students' union premises) is not denied to anyone because of their beliefs or politics.'

Chapter 12
78 Patrick Johnstone, *Operation World* (Paternoster and WEC International; editions regularly updated).

Acknowledgments

From Oliver Barclay

This book cannot pretend to be a piece of thorough research – in its account of the first 100 years or the following twenty-five. It depends heavily on secondary sources and in particular on J. C. Pollock's *A Cambridge Movement*. I am deeply indebted to Mr Pollock for his permission to quote extensively from that book. To the wide-ranging research that Mr Pollock has done I have added in certain areas only. My conclusions are not always identical with Pollock's, but anyone who reads both books will quickly see that some chapters rely extensively on his work.

My only claim to be able to write such a history is that, although I am not a historian, I have had unique contact with the CICCU over a considerable slice of its history. My father and mother and their brothers and other friends were all involved in their time (1876–1905). I have known personally a representative group of those who were leaders in the CICCU since 1895 and myself had the privilege of being up from 1938 to 1945. I have also had fairly continuous involvement with the CICCU ever since. I therefore have to acknowledge my debt to a large number of former CICCU members of all generations who have talked about their time at Cambridge and have sometimes shown me documents from the time that they were students.

A number of people read parts of the manuscript in draft and made invaluable comments. My wife tackled the most difficult task of all, which was to transcribe my original manuscript into legible type, and without her help it would have been difficult to finish the job. So many people have given information, advice and criticism that I cannot list them all.

From both authors

Finally we both acknowledge our debt to the contemporaries who constituted the CICCU of our day. Like everyone else who has been caught up in its life, we confess how much we owe to its ongoing influence. To write this history has been a fresh reminder of how much we have all owed to that group of raw but spiritually privileged fellow students, mostly a year or so older than ourselves, who set an example and gave us a vision for Christian living and Christian witness at Cambridge. That is to say, we all have to confess how much we owe to a remarkable work of God in the lives of men and women and to those friends who demonstrated it.

Chief sources

A. There are two major sources that cover much of the ground up to 1910 and 1952 respectively. Most of the quotations for which no other reference is given come from Pollock.

Tissington Tatlow, *The Story of the Student Christian Movement of Great Britain and Ireland* (SCM Press, 1933).

J. C. Pollock, *A Cambridge Movement* (John Murray, 1953).

B. Other printed books and pamphlets:

G. R. Balleine, *A History of the Evangelical Party in the Church of England* (Longmans Green, 1908).

Oliver R. Barclay, *Evangelicalism in Britain 1935–1995: A Personal Sketch* (IVP, 1997).

B. Godfrey Buxton, *The Reward of Faith in the Life of Barclay Fowell Buxton 1860–1946* (Lutterworth Press, 1949).

CICCU, *Old Paths in Perilous Times* (Marshall, Morgan and Scott, 1913; 2nd edn, IVF, 1933).

F. D. Coggan (ed.), *Christ and the Colleges: A History of the*

Inter-Varsity Fellowship of Evangelical Unions (IVFEU, 1934).

W. R. T. Gairdner, *D. M. Thornton: A Study in Missionary Ideals and Methods* (Hodder and Stoughton, 1908).

Norman P. Grubb, *C. T. Studd: Cricketer and Pioneer* (Lutterworth Press, 1933).

C. F. Harford-Battersby, *Pilkington of Uganda* (Marshall Brothers, no date).

Adrian Hastings, *A History of English Christianity 1920–1985* (Collins Fount, 1986).

Risto Lehtonen, *Story of a Storm: The Ecumenical Student Movement in the Turmoil of Revolution* (Eerdmans, 1998).

Marcus L. Loane, *Archbishop Mowll: The Biography of H. W. K. Mowll* (Hodder and Stoughton, 1960).

Basil Matthews, *John R. Mott, World Citizen* (SCM Press, 1934).

Handley C. G. Moule, *Charles Simeon* (1892; reissued IVF, 1948).

Handley C. G. Moule, *Thoughts on Christian Sanctity* (Seeley, 1885).

C. Padwick, *Temple Gairdner of Cairo* (SPCK, 1929).

J. C. Pollock, *The Cambridge Seven* (IVF, 1955).

E. Porter, *Victorian Cambridge* (Dennis Dobson, 1969).

Ruth Rouse, *The World Student Christian Federation* (SCM Press, 1948).

Eugene Stock, *The History of the Church Missionary Society*, vols. I–III (CMS, 1899).

Oliver Tomkins, *The Life of Edward Woods* (SCM Press, 1957).

Max Warren, *Crowded Canvas: Some Experiences of a Lifetime* (Hodder and Stoughton, 1974).

Robert P. Wilder, *The Great Commission* (Oliphants, 1936).

Robert P. Wilder, *The Student Volunteer Movement* (SVM, 1938).

E. S. Woods and F. B. MacNutt, *Theodore, Bishop of Winchester: A Memoir of Frank Theodore Woods 1874–1932* (SPCK, 1933).

A Brief History of the Inter-Varsity Fellowship of Evangelical Christian Unions (IVFECU, c. 1928).

Fundamentalism: A Religious Problem. Letters to the Editor of The Times *and a Leading Article* (Times Publishing, 1955).

C. Other sources not detailed in the Notes:

CICCU records.

The personal diaries of David B. Barclay for 1897, 1898, 1899.

Dr Basil Atkinson's 1996 handwritten memorandum entitled 'Basil's Recollections'. About four copies were made and one is in the UCCF Office.

Cambridge University Missionary Band prayer letters.

Personal discussions and correspondence, some of it tape-recorded, with Godfrey Buxton, Joe Church, Norman Grubb, Kenneth Hooker, Noel Palmer and a number of others.

Written memoranda by a considerable number of CICCU leaders for the periods 1953–73 and 1976–2002.

Mr Ben Harder, at the time a research student at Aberdeen and later Professor of Church History in the Graduate Department of Winnipeg Bible College, Canada; he provided a number of scripts of interviews and copies of material from the SCM archives. He had obtained these in connection with his own researches on the period up to 1910.

J. C. Pollock, *A Cambridge Movement*, gives further extensive references, some of which have been consulted.

Index